NEW LIFE
IN THE SPIRIT

BY

LEONARD I. SWEET

THE WESTMINSTER PRESS
PHILADELPHIA

BOOK DESIGN BY ALICE DERR

First edition

Published by The Westminster Press®
Philadelphia, Pennsylvania

PRINTED IN THE UNITED STATES OF AMERICA
9 8 7 6 5 4 3 2 1

Library of Congress Cataloging in Publication Data

Sweet, Leonard I.
  New life in the Spirit.

  (Library of living faith)
  Bibliography: p.
  1. Holy Spirit. I. Title. II. Series.
BT121.2.S94   231'.3   81-23112
ISBN 0-664-24414-9   AACR2

CONTENTS

FOREWORD

The word "theology" comes from two Greek words—*theos* ("God") and *logos* ("word" or "thought"). Theology is simply words about God or thinking about God. But for many Christians, theology is remote, abstract, baffling, confusing, and boring. They turn it over to the professionals—the theologians—who can ponder and inquire into the ways of God with the world.

This series, Library of Living Faith, is for those Christians who thought theology wasn't for them. It is a collection of ten books on crucial doctrines or issues in the Christian faith today. Each book attempts to show why our theology—our thoughts about God—matters in what we do and say as Christians. The series is an invitation to readers to become theologians themselves—to reflect on the Bible and on the history of the church and to find their own ways of understanding the grace of God in Jesus Christ.

The Library of Living Faith is in the tradition of another series published by Westminster Press in the 1950s, the Layman's Theological Library. This new collection of volumes tries to serve the church in the challenges of the closing decades of this century.

The ten books are based on the affirmation of the Letter to the Ephesians (4:4–6): "There is one body and one Spirit, just as you were called to the one hope that belongs to your call, one Lord, one faith, one baptism, one God and Father of us all, who is above all and through all and in all." Each book addresses a particular theme as part of the

Christian faith as a whole; each book speaks to the church as a whole. Theology is too important to be left only to the theologians; it is the work and witness of the entire people of God.

But, as Ephesians says, "grace was given to each of us according to the measure of Christ's gift" (Eph. 4:7), and the Library of Living Faith tries to demonstrate the diversity of theology in the church today. Differences, of course, are not unique to American Christianity. One only needs to look at the New Testament and the early church to see how "the measure of Christ's gift" produced disagreement and conflict as well as a rich variety of understandings of Christian faith and discipleship. In the midst of the unity of the faith, there has never been uniformity. The authors in this series have their own points of view, and readers may argue along the way with the authors' interpretations. But each book presents varying points of view and shows what difference it makes to take a particular theological position. Sparks may fly, but the result, we hope, will be a renewed vision of what it means to be a Christian exhibiting in the world today a living faith.

These books are also intended to be a library—a set of books that should be read together. Of course, not everything is included. As the Gospel of John puts it, "There are also many other things which Jesus did; were every one of them to be written I suppose that the world itself could not contain the books that would be written" (John 21:25). Readers should not be content to read just the volume on Jesus Christ or on God or on the Holy Spirit and leave out those on the church or on the Christian life or on Christianity's relationship with other faiths. For we are called to one faith with many parts.

The volumes are also designed to be read by groups of people. Writing may be a lonely task, but the literature of the church was never intended for individuals alone. It is for the entire body of Christ. Through discussion and even debate, the outlines of a living faith can emerge.

The concept of the Holy Spirit may be the most fascinating and yet the most elusive doctrine in Christian theology. In this book, Leonard I. Sweet discusses the central place that the Holy Spirit should occupy in the life and mission of the church. Dr. Sweet is a United Methodist pastor who also serves on the faculties of the University of Rochester and Colgate Rochester Divinity School/Bexley Hall/Crozer Theological Seminary. He was born and raised in the Holiness tradition of American Protestantism, but his mother's lipstick and his father's television set prompted them to migrate to the United Methodist Church, where Dr. Sweet has been ever since. His interests are wide-ranging, for he describes himself as "a historian who is also a compulsive tire-kicker in the parking lots of theology and psychology." He is the author of *Black Images of America, 1784–1870* (1976), *Women in the Ministry: The Minister's Wife in American Religion* (forthcoming), and many articles, essays, and reviews.

JOHN M. MULDER

Louisville Presbyterian Theological Seminary
Louisville, Kentucky

ACKNOWLEDGMENTS

Ideas for this book were first tried out on "Dove's Disciples," an adult School of Religion class organized by David Parish, the Education Chairperson of the Geneseo United Methodist Church. This fervent and faithful group (Deb Angiolillo, Evelyn Forth, Margaret Goodridge, Leslie and Helge Heen, Deb Henry, Sue Holler, Betty J. Keller, Luella and Ron Krahl, Betty Olmsted, Pat and Chad Putnam, Linda Scoville, and Bev Young) met for a year in each other's homes where they tested my experiments, tossed around my probings, and threw back an improved understanding of the Holy Spirit. Most significantly, they unwittingly modeled what a community of the Spirit looks, acts, and feels like.

My reflections on the Spirit have been undeservedly nourished by continuing stimulation from three colleagues at Colgate Rochester/Bexley Hall/Crozer, Charles M. Nielsen, Beverly Roberts Gaventa, and J. Stephen Pembridge, and by four pastoral colleagues in the Rochester area, Manfred Lassen, C. Frederick Yoos, Susan S. Shafer, and Theodore J. Weeden, Sr. Al Parnell helped arrange for a couple extra weeks of study leave from the church so I could finish the manuscript, Edith and Philip Ditzel offered an ideal setting at Conesus Lake where writing could take place, and Connie Johnston honored a large draft on her time, trouble, and typing. My brother John David Sweet, a Presbyterian pastor in Philadelphia, suffered some extended suppertime phone calls to help me find my way through

11

a section luxuriant with trouble. John Mulder, general editor of the series, was always there with words of counsel "fitly spoken." The daily acts of forbearance and kindness extended by my wife, Joan, and two sons, Leonard Jr. and Justin, are beyond imagining.

But most of all I thank my mother, Mabel Boggs Sweet, for first encouraging me to ride the "wings of the wind." I dedicate this book to her, and in memory of my father, Leonard Lucius Sweet.

INTRODUCTION

It is a pleasure not to have to begin a book on the Holy Spirit by decrying the neglect of this doctrine in the church's life and thought. One of America's premier preachers, David H. C. Read, published a sermon in 1971 entitled "The Holy Spirit in Hiding." How quickly times can change. No longer can it be said of the church that it has kept the Holy Spirit behind closed doors. The emphasis on the Holy Spirit is one of the greatest religious developments in the past twenty years.

Karl Barth's conviction that the main agenda for modern theology should be the doctrine of the Spirit is being carried out. One of the most pronounced features of our time is the study of the Holy Spirit. Not since the Puritans has there been such attention given to "the Unknown God," "the Half-known God," the "Dark Continent" of the Christian life (Arthur Hird), "the theologians' stepchild" (Emil Brunner), or the "Cinderella doctrine" of theology (G. K. Sirks). The fundamental questions of theology (study of God) and christology (study of Jesus) have been replaced in the 1970s by pneumatology (study of Holy Spirit). In fact, the ratio in the Apostles' Creed of ten articles on christology to one article on pneumatology has been almost reversed in recent books and periodicals. Theologians have rediscovered the Spirit. So too, it appears, have some scientists. Werner Heisenberg questions in *Physics and Philosophy* (1958) whether theological words like "God" and "Spirit" may not convey the truth of reality more clearly than scientific concepts.

So why another book on the Holy Spirit? One is tempted to say with Mae West, "Too much of a good thing is—wonderful." But it goes deeper than that. Much of the renewed emphasis on Pentecost among contemporary Christians has taken place either in Pentecostal denominations or in parachurch functions. Mainline churches are still by and large suffering from the "two's company, three's a crowd" syndrome, with Pentecost crowding a church calendar that revolves around Christmas and Easter. In previous periods of history, churches were known to celebrate Pentecost Sunday with great pageantry and blaring trumpets, or more dangerously with "Whitsun ale," roses raining down from the rafters on the heads of the congregation, or doves released from the roof swooping throughout the sanctuary during the service. Today the pastor who merely decorates the church on Pentecost Sunday with geraniums and asks the congregation to wear red is the talk of the town.

Even where Pentecost is in perpetual observance there is all too often a lack of theological rigor. Experience and understanding are two different things. One does not have to be like the converts at Ephesus who scratched their heads in puzzlement when Paul asked them about the Holy Spirit ("We have never even heard that there is a Holy Spirit"—Acts 19:2) to identify with the ritual quotation of the convert from Shintoism to Christianity who confessed to the missionary: "Most High Person of Honorable Father, him I understand. Honorable Son, him also I understand. But please be so favorable as to tell me, who is that Honorable Bird?" The most prevalent invocation of the Holy Spirit is still a rhetorical employment which signals to a congregation that the end of whatever they are doing is near.

A main reason why our understanding of the Spirit can be shallow even when our experience may be deep hit home one day as I conversed with a Doctor of Ministry student. He stated that he never preached to his congregation on the doctrine of the Holy Spirit, because they couldn't understand it. It is little wonder that many Christian minds have not given ten minutes of thought in the last ten years to a subject like the Trinity. Churches characterized by what Karl Barth called a "flat-tire" Christianity (one with the Spirit gone out of it) often have their pastors to thank for not blowing them up when they needed it.

One risks a great deal in writing about the Holy Spirit. After all, what more can one say about the wind than that it blows where it wills? For the same reason that we do not pray *to* the Holy Spirit, but pray *in, of,* and *by* the Holy Spirit, we cannot adequately write about the Holy Spirit. Or as Dorothy Sayers confessed in frustration, "We cannot really look at the movement of the Spirit, just because it is the power by which we do the looking." Yet many good books have been written recently about the Spirit that enrich and extend both our experience and our understanding of God.

This book is only a gentle introduction to this literature and to the topic. It contains no piercing new discoveries, many unconcluded thoughts. I have borrowed like a magpie, and the ideas I have that are worth having are inspired by the insights of others. What Cyril of Jerusalem wrote in his *Catecheses* I feel deeply: "The grace of the Spirit is truly necessary if we want to deal with the Holy Spirit; not that we may speak adequately about Him—for that is impossible—but that we may pass through this subject without danger, by saying what the divine Scriptures contain." But if anyone spiritually sunburned from exposure to the Spirit because of excessive theological nudity is drawn inside to put on some garments of understanding, or if anyone spiritually anemic from a shuttered, "paper" piety is lured outdoors to experience firsthand the invigorating rays of the Spirit, the risks will have been worth taking.

1
THE POWER
OF THE SPIRIT

"You shall receive power when the Holy Spirit has come upon you" (Acts 1:8). What the Holy Spirit is about is power: power to make whole, power to make alive, power to bring together, power to put down the mighty from their seats, power to exalt the lowly and meek. There is no evidence that any Christians were added to the faith between Easter and Pentecost. Why? The talk was there, but not the power. We can proclaim Christ crucified all we want, we can trumpet the glad tidings of a risen and regnant Lord, but without the power of the Holy Spirit, there will be no healing of brokenness, no release of forgiveness, no surge of vitality, no unleashing of lives. "The kingdom of God does not consist in talk but in power" (I Cor. 4:20). If no transcendent power accompanies the gospel, evangelism is both insincere and vain. The Holy Spirit is the source of all transforming acts in Christian history. Indeed, the book of Acts has sometimes been called not "The Acts of the Apostles" but "The Acts of the Holy Spirit."

We need to be careful about what kind of "power" we are talking about. As Bertrand Russell, Alfred Adler, and others have emphasized, the will to power is one of the driving forces of our day—driving us often to our destruction. It was not so different in Jesus' time. In Acts 8:9–24 there appears a man by the name of Simon, a magician. When Simon saw what the Holy Spirit could do, he offered Peter money and exclaimed, "Give me also this power." He wanted the Spirit because of the power. He received from Peter one of the more powerful rebukes in the New Testament because of his spirit. The lust in Simon's eyes blinded him to the true nature of the Spirit's power. The power of the Holy Spirit is not something you can hold; it is something that holds you. It is not a possession. It is a pilgrimage.

The Spirit opens and closes the Bible. Between Gen. 1:2 and Rev. 22:17 a multitude of metaphors are presented to symbolize God's Spirit. Out of this abundance of riches (some have found as many as fifty-two different names for the Spirit in the Bible) I have selected five of the most familiar and provocative names to help us clarify what kind of power God's Spirit represents. These are not exhaustive but suggestive for your own travel through the Scriptures, perhaps with the concordance entry on "power" as your guide. "Wind" is the creative power of the Spirit. "Oil" is the comforting power of the Spirit. "Fire" is the purifying power of the Spirit. "Dove" is the suffering power of the Spirit. And "water" is the life-giving power of the Spirit.

These categories are not always separable. They often overlap. Wind, fire, water suggest the inescapable, dynamic, and unpredictable qualities of a Spirit that is as gentle or as violent as fire that warms the hands or burns buildings, wind that fans the face or rips off rooftops, water that refreshes the body or floods cities. Oil joins them in connoting a flowing, engulfing presence. The dove, the only bodily shape for the Holy Spirit, suggests concreteness and grace. Some theologians, like J. Robert Nelson, shun such images because they minimize the personality of the Holy Spirit and are guilty of a "distorting, diminishing, and trivializing of the power of the Divine Reality." The grain of truth to this argument is offset by the bushels of biblical references to the Spirit in these terms. Wind, oil, fire, dove, water is the Bible's vocabulary for the Spirit "of power, and of love, and of a sound mind" (II Tim. 1:7, KJV).

The most common biblical words for "Spirit" are *ruach* (Hebrew) and *pneuma* (Greek). Each suggests air that is constantly in motion—"wind," "breath"—and each can be found over three hundred times in the Old and New Testaments. Perhaps the classic Old Testament description of the creative power of God's Spirit is the exciting "valley of dry bones" passage in Ezekiel (37:1–14). The problem with this vivid tale of God breathing into nostrils and making them into noses is that it suggests that God's Spirit is a creative power that brings all creation to life. There are a handful of passages (e.g., Ps. 104:29) that tolerate such an interpretation. But other passages right in Ezekiel (36:26; cf. 11:19–20) and in the thirty-nine places in the Old Testament where *ruach* is employed as an agent of God give a fuller understanding of the kind of life the winds of God's Spirit create. The truer biblical insight is that God's Spirit is less a power that creates living things and more a power that makes living things create—that makes *Homo sapiens* become a living, creating soul; that energizes judges, prophets, artists, and kings to act and speak with new vitality and insight; that embraces relationships and moves them in unforeseen directions.

Theologians have differentiated between two ways the Spirit's creative power blows in the wind: as an indwelling, as an invasion. God's indwelling Spirit is that creative power which "breathes" through us the divine life and inspires our living with divine truth and beauty. God's Spirit breathed through the people of Israel, inspiring arts and crafts, raising heroes, animating the souls of those chosen for special assignments. The same power that coursed through the New Testament writers when they preached breathed through them when they wrote. "All Scripture is God-breathed" is how II Tim. 3:16 literally reads. Breathing is natural, free, and different for each person. So it is for everyone who is alive with the indwelling Spirit. Breathing is unconscious; we don't think about it. When we do, we can hyperventilate—which is what happens spiritually to some Christians when they focus on the respiration instead of the application of the Spirit. Breath also blows hot and cold, hot on our bare hands to keep them warm in winter, cold on our hot soup to cool it down. So also the winds of God's creative power blow hot and cold. Ask any writer.

But sometimes God's Spirit invades from without. Without wind, our ancestors would not have known of other lands, of other cultures, of other horizons. Without the Spirit of the God who rides the "wings of the wind" (II Sam. 22:11), we could not be stirred to soar above ourselves. Invading winds may be as gentle as a cool evening breeze or as violent as a gale. We like it best when creative power comes as a still, soft whisper of wind—safe, quiet, orderly. But the Bible indicates that sometimes the Spirit activates creativity with the force of a rushing mighty wind—ambushing our lives with surprise, confusion, noise, and uncertainty. Whether these violent gusts knock us down or carry us forward depends on whether we chart our lives so that we sail with the wind or against it.

We are afraid to go very far with the wind for fear of where we might be taken. It feels safer and easier to be swept along by the winds of the world than to stand up to these currents of conformism that often beat against those who would "walk in the Spirit." But the creative winds of the Spirit want to make each of us an original. "Without form and void" is a good description of a lot of people. They get in shape only by running with the crowd. The pressure is intense to make Christians more and more like their surroundings and to make Christians more and more like each other. But a conformist spirit is not the Holy Spirit.

When I feel especially squeezed by the gates of the world—which, by the time one gets through them, end up being narrower and straighter than the gates of faith—I have a kind of mantra which I repeat: *"Christianus sum."* These words first came alive during a chat I had with a pastor in his office before I was to speak to an adult education class. I noticed a wall plaque inscribed with the Latin words *"Christianus sum,"* and a name and the dates "1967–1977." I was interested in the story behind the plaque, having named our youngest son after Justin Martyr, the early Christian philosopher who was beheaded about A.D. 165 after being examined by the Roman prefect Rusticus. Justin's defiant declaration *"Christianus sum"* ("I am a Christian") carried with it the sentence of death. The pastor related that the plaque had been given to him by the parents of a ten-year-old boy who died of cancer. As the boy's mother was rushing him to the hospital for what would prove to be his last admission, a car darted out in front of them. Slamming on her brakes, she screamed at her son, "Why don't you curse that car for me." "I can't, mom," he replied. "I am a Christian."

The *"Christianus sum"* spirit is less difficult for us to maintain than for Justin Martyr or the ten-year-old boy. But it is still not easy. Industrial societies increasingly demand higher levels of conformity from their members and display lower toleration thresholds for personal quirks and eccentricities that cut against the common grain. Michel Foucault's lifetime of scholarship chronicles the ways in which modern societies twist the handles on the vice of coercion, regimentation, and repressiveness until everyone looks, acts, eats, feels, and thinks like everyone else. Those who differ from the standardized dream are shunned, segregated, confined, or constrained.

The marks of conformism are showing among those who should only fear lack of conformity to Christ. Is God so unimaginative that he patterns all Christians in the same mold? It is not just the cults that seem to think so. But the creative power of the Spirit gives each person's life unique shape and style. The winds of the Spirit do not whip Christians into homogenized communities with a smooth, creamy faith of uniform conversions, theologies, and behavior. The consistency of a Christian community is lumpy, with lots of pulp and chunks that are sometimes hard to swallow. The first of ten consequences of being filled with the Spirit that revivalist Charles G. Finney listed in his classic *Lectures on Revivals of Religion* (1835) was: "You will be called eccentric; and probably you will deserve it. Probably you will really be eccentric. I never knew a person who was filled with the Spirit, that was not eccentric." Besides a mind, a soul, a body, and a Bible, every properly equipped Christian must have a character that distinguishes him or her as an original. It was this uniqueness that moved Ralph Waldo Emerson to exclaim: "A new person is to me a great event and hinders me from sleep."

The Holy Spirit blows whither he wills, creating characters out of conformists, fanning the smoldering sparks of individuality within until the flame of originality glows. The Russian word for freedom, *swoboda,* is made up of two roots which mean "be myself." The creative wind of the Spirit frees us to be ourselves without fear or guilt. If God made you a simple person, you don't have to try to be a complex one. If God made you with a swinging beat, you don't have to like "I Come to the Garden Alone." If God made you a square, you don't have to imitate the eggheads. "To know what you prefer," Robert Louis Stevenson wrote, "instead of humbly saying 'Amen' to what the world tells you you ought to prefer, is to have kept your soul alive."

The paradox is that the Holy Spirit unites as he diversifies, and the stronger the community, the more differences there will be in the people who make it up. If the Holy Spirit did not create characters, we would not have a Christian community at all but a collectivity, a hive of identical and interchangeable believers who buzz about in the same smiles and styles, drone on endlessly the same slogans, and sting into submission or retreat all outsiders who would penetrate too deeply into their cell-like chambers. When Christians begin to exhibit common kinds of behavior and stereotypical symptoms, there is an indication of spiritual illness in the community. Healthy Christians all act differently.

Oil symbolizes the comforting power of the Spirit, with "comforting" defined as "strengthening for service." Moses poured oil over Aaron's head, beard, and robe, consecrating him for service (Lev. 8:12; Ps. 133:1–2). Samuel anointed David with oil, authenticating his selection by God as one who was to perform great duties (I Sam. 16:13). Elijah anointed kings and prophets with oil, setting them apart for special responsibilities. When Jesus' public ministry began, the text he chose for his first sermon was the anointing passage from Isa. 61:1 (Luke 4:18; cf. Acts 4:27; 10:38). Ever since Pentecost, the oil of God's Spirit has been running down, sanctifying for service—not just on select individuals, but on all Christians. This does not happen just once. There is a fresh anointing for every new task.

If "Thou anointest my head with oil" conveys a message of service, "Thy rod and thy staff they comfort me" tells of strengthening. Bible translators have not known what to do with the Greek word for the Holy Spirit, *parakletos*. This word, sometimes referred to as "Paraclete," is variously translated "Counselor," "Advocate," "Helper," and "the God who stands by you." The King James Version still renders it best as "Comforter," a word which comes from two old English words that mean "strengthen greatly." "Comforter" should not convey the weak notion of a soft, woolly blanket that wraps around infants to keep them warm—although that is the sad expectation of too many Christians about the Holy Spirit. When the Holy Spirit comes upon us, he makes us strong. When the Spirit came upon him, Samson tore a lion to pieces (Judg. 14:5–6). When Luke explains how the early church was built up "in the comfort of the Holy Spirit" (Acts 9:31), he is referring to the Spirit's power, not to soothe and console, but to fortify and serve. Early Bible translators Wycliffe and Tyndale associated "comfort" and "Comforter" with words like ennoblement, upholding, and pith. The Puritans commonly named their children "Comfort" (in the King James Version, the meaning of the name "Noah" is thus translated— Gen. 5:29). According to a midrash on the Old Testament text, Noah invented history's first machine and thereby strengthened human ability to enjoy and handle life.

Roy Pearson tells of an old tapestry depicting William the Conqueror urging his troops into battle by presenting the point of his sword to their posteriors. The caption reads: "William Comforts His Soldiers." The Holy Spirit goads us in our struggle for truth and joins with us in our battle against evil. The comforting power of the Spirit turns our face to the world and strengthens us for service.

The burning bush, the pillar of fire, the Mt. Carmel altar, the Pentecost flame—all signify enormous earthspots of divine presence. Fire is the most alluring, and the most menacing, of all the symbols of the Holy Spirit. The drowsy melodies of the crackling fire it took you an hour to light in the fireplace can become—when somebody else only flicks a cigarette butt—a death song, transforming a forest into a funeral pyre.

John the Baptist called Jesus the one who "will baptize you with the Holy Spirit and with fire" (Matt. 3:11; Luke 3:16). Many commentators have seen the "fire" as an apocalyptic reference to Judgment Day. Judgment Day is not only a day but, as Franz Kafka observed, a "court in perpetual session." The purifying power of fire constantly judges the world, burning down all that stands in the way of a new creation, welding "characters" into communities afire for justice and peace, scorching the last jot of luke-warmness from our souls, and kindling our spirits into living flames that burn and sometimes burn out with a passion for humanity. As one of my parishioners whom I have tried to slow down says to me, "I would rather leave behind on this earth a pile of ashes than a pile of dust." From dust we came, but to ashes Christians return.

There is a story about a Pentecost celebration staged by fifteenth-century Italian ruler Lorenzo de' Medici ("Lorenzo the Magnificent") that illustrates this, although I have been unable to verify its historical accuracy. In one of Florence's magnificent cathedrals, a system of wires and pulleys coming down from the ceiling was supposedly designed so that real fire would come streaking down over the heads of the congregation. Everything worked as planned until the fire brushed against some flimsy curtains and ignited them. The church burned to the ground. The purifying power of the Spirit fights fire with fire. It counters threatening fires of destruction with the fire of the Spirit, burning unholy structures, even churches, to the ground, setting the world on fire.

Although it is found in all four Gospels at Jesus' baptism, the dove's identification with the Holy Spirit does not have a strong biblical basis. Yet until the Middle Ages, the dove was almost the exclusive representation of the Holy Spirit. Its durability has been in some measure due to the dove's association with vulnerability and suffering. The sacrifice of a dove was required in the Jewish initiatory rite for proselytes, and Jewish parents of a male child gave a traditional thanksgiving offering of a lamb and a dove, although Mary and Joseph were so poor that when they presented Jesus at the Temple for the first time all they could afford were two turtle doves (Luke 2:22ff.). There is no chirpy cheerfulness in the coo of this bird of sacrifice. The dove stands apart from other birds in the piercing note of sadness in its cry and its use of speed and agility instead of talons and thrusts to rise above conflict. When the dove swoops down, it is not as a bird of prey but as a bird of peace. The tale of the suffering power of the dove is the old story of overcoming evil with good, hatred with love, suffering with suffering.

When it comes to our grasping for power, we are still back in the Garden of Eden, biting on the apple. The dominant concept of power today revolves around money, muscle, multitudes, and might. The Christian concept of power revolves around suffering. Bernard Loomer has written a most stimulating discussion on the difference between the power of the world and the power of the Spirit. He says that human life has been characterized by "unilateral power"— the ability to control, influence, and force people to do things. The exercise of "unilateral power" alienates and isolates people, turns them into objects, and abolishes mystery and freedom.

The Spirit, however, calls us to "relational power"—that is, "the capacity both to influence others and to be influenced by others"; the power, not to force others to change, but to move others to change; the authority of relationships characterized by openness, presence, suffering, and vulnerability where others are not seen as extensions of one's needs but as people of creative freedom themselves. Loomer concludes: "Jesus, who is to be found at the bottom of the hierarchy of unilateral power, stands at the apex of life conceived in terms of relational power."

The power of the Holy Spirit derives from the cross and resurrection, from the weak things of this world, from "defenselessness" (Hendrikus Berkhof), from suffering love. The most powerful weapon on earth is the suffering love of the dove. When Malcolm Muggeridge interviewed the Soviet dissident Christian Anatole Kusnyetsov, he inquired how his soul could be so on fire for God in a glacial climate of persecution. He replied: "If in this world you are confronted with absolute power, power unmitigated, power unrestrained, extending to every area of human life—if you are confronted with power in those terms, you are driven to realize that the only possible response to it is not some alternative power arrangement, more humane, more enlightened. The only possible response to absolute power is the absolute love which our Lord brought into this world."

Jesus was not killed because he was a "powerful" man. He had none of the "unilateral" forms of power—no weapons, no money, no academic authority, no masses of disciples. By the standards of the potentates of the world he was "powerless." But Jesus was killed because some powerful authorities sensed he had the greatest power in the universe behind him—the suffering power of the Spirit that can draw strength and peace out of weakness and relationships.

We associate water with the womb's gift of intelligent life, faith's gift of abundant life (John 7:38), and Jesus' gift of new life (Matt. 18:3). Water is the source and sustainer of life; it symbolizes the life-giving power of the Spirit.

But it is with Jesus that the Holy Spirit's life-giving power becomes indissolubly linked. The Spirit's life-giving power is what made Jesus come alive to earth (see Gabriel's words to Mary in Luke 1:35). It made Jesus' mission come alive at the Jordan River (Matt. 3:16). It makes Jesus come alive now as more than a model or memory and become for us "the living past" (Michael Ramsey). And it gives life to the Scriptures as they witness to God's revelation in Jesus Christ. Since the coming of Christ, there has been a gradual going away of the impersonal imagery for God's Spirit.

How it must have hurt the disciples to hear Jesus' valedictory words to them: "It is good for you that I go away" (John 16:7). They could not imagine what he was talking about, because during Jesus' earthly ministry the disciples had not yet received the Holy Spirit (John 7:39) and because Jesus seldom instructed them in the subject of the Spirit. They could not have known that whenever he taught them about the kingdom he was really teaching them about God's Spirit. Only gradually did the early Christians come out of the dark tunnel of uncertainty about the work of the Holy Spirit—the first light they related to Jesus' resurrection (Rom. 1:4), then as the light grew brighter they related the Spirit to Jesus' baptism and ministry (Mark 1:10), and finally to Jesus' conception (Luke 1:35). In short, the full ramifications of what Jesus meant when he said that the Spirit's descent awaited his ascent were not immediately clear to the disciples.

Augustine may be right in claiming that Pentecost is improperly celebrated as the "birthday of the Holy Spirit," for the Holy Spirit had been present before—but only selectively and temporarily, a divine draping that occasionally mantled some figure to perform unusual service. No matter how much his disciples might have wanted to cling to his presence, Jesus insisted that it was to their advantage that he go away, because the Holy Spirit would come and universalize his ministry. The body of Jesus never left Palestine; the Spirit of Jesus spread throughout the world, as the early church, through the power of the Holy Spirit, preached Jesus—whose life revealed faith, whose death revealed love, and whose resurrection revealed hope.

This was Paul's great departure from previous views of God's Spirit. New Testament scholar Paul Meyer writes: "While there is little distinctively Christian about either the language about the Holy Spirit or the notions of Spirit found even in Paul, *these become distinctively Christian precisely when they are related, and by virtue of being related, to the figure of Jesus Christ.*" Just as God was incarnate in Christ, so Christ would now become incarnate in the Christian community through the power of the Holy Spirit. The Holy Spirit is what makes Christ a living Christ. The backdrop for the coming of the Spirit, according to Acts 2, was a sermon on the resurrection of Jesus. It is the life-giving power of the Holy Spirit, as Luther insisted, that lifts Jesus out of the grave of history and makes him become present and alive to us through justification and sanctification.

The Holy Spirit always strives for anonymity and transparency, pointing to and clarifying the revelation given by Jesus Christ. When Paul discovered that the Ephesians did not know about the Holy Spirit, he did not immediately teach them the Holy Spirit. He taught them Christ (Acts 19:1–7). Were the Spirit to break away from Christ and go on his own, the truth of God would become fogged with the mists of our imagination and subjectivity.

2
THE DIVINITY
OF THE SPIRIT

As we begin this chapter let us take off our shoes, for we are entering sacred chambers. "The mystery of the Holy Trinity is the central mystery of Christianity," writes Herbert Mühlen. Yet this is the point where lay people, and many theologians as well, walk out on theology. When is the last time time you heard a sermon or read a book on the Trinity? Have you ever celebrated Trinity Sunday or even Pentecost with as much verve and fanfare as you celebrate Christmas and Easter? It is hard for us to imagine whatever possessed some American colonies to enact laws making "any reproachful speeches concerning the Holy Trinity" punishable by death.

One reason we hesitate to venture into the mysteries of the Trinity is that it is the twilight zone of theology. We readily identify with the young German Reformer Philip Melanchthon, who was dismayed at the celestial calculus of "one in three and three in one," concluding: "We adore the mysteries of the Godhead. That is better than to investigate them." Even the great creeds of the faith are better seen as grand hymns to the Trinity than as doctrinal formulations. The Nicene Creed, John Calvin observed, is "more of a hymn suited for singing than a formula of confession." We can only answer the great question of the Trinity with a sputter and whisper. The best we can do is praise.

Second, as the Spanish theologian Michael Servetus—who was burned at the stake in 1553—found out, it is difficult to speak about the Trinity without getting into

trouble. "Of the wise men among us," Gregory of Nazianzus wrote, "some consider the Spirit as an activity, some as
a creature, some as God; and some have not known which
of these things to choose, a reverence, as they say, for
scripture, as if it made no clear declarations." But that is
precisely the problem, for the Bible does not make clear
declarations about the Trinity and it is vague about the
Spirit. We do not step from the vigorous unitarian pages of
the Old Testament into staunchly trinitarian pages of the
New Testament. The word "Trinity" is not found in the
Bible, and in all the Synoptic Gospels there is only one
trinitarian passage (Matt. 28:19), and this is liturgical rather
than theological. The primitive creedal formula in I Cor.
8:6 and the christological hymns of Philippians and Colos-
sians completely ignore the Spirit. Jesus seldom spoke of
the Holy Spirit (Matt. 12:28; 28:19; Mark 13:11 and parallels; Luke 4:18; 11:13; 12:10; and parallels), and the Bible
is reluctant to speak of the Holy Spirit as God.

Clearly, trinitarian issues were not of pressing concern to
the New Testament writers. When we do find references to
the Holy Spirit in the apostolic church, the Spirit is never
called God and is most often identified with the spirit of
God, the spirit of the preexistent Christ, or the inspirer of
the prophets. The doctrine of the Holy Spirit took a back
seat to the person and work of Christ during the first three
centuries, and from the scanty references to the Holy Spirit
in the ancient church, one marvels that Christianity ever
developed along trinitarian lines. If the doctrine of the
Holy Spirit was not the first example of progressive revelation, it was a close second.

At the same time the apostolic age was "binitarian," it
lavishly records testimony to the reality and presence of the
Holy Spirit in the life of the church—and it is on this raw
experience that trinitarian doctrine rests. The apostolic
church witnessed a plurality of four opinions on the Holy
Spirit: (1) an attribute of God; (2) a divine gift; (3) an
impersonal force; (4) a distinct person in the Godhead. The
Christian tradition did not officially resolve these divergent
views until late in the fourth century, and the Holy Spirit

was not examined on a level equal to that given the Father and Son until the early fifth century (Augustine's great *De Trinitate*). The Council of Nicaea (325) identified Christ as equal to God. But "at Nicea the doctrine of the Holy Spirit"—Jaroslav Pelikan writes—"had been disposed of in lapidary brevity: 'And [we believe] in the Holy Spirit.' " It remained for the Council of Constantinople (381) to say that the Holy Spirit is equal to God. It would be hard to find a theologian before Constantinople who would not have suffered the same fate as Servetus if judged by the same exacting standards of dogma.

In Helen Waddell's novel *Peter Abelard* (1933), the canon of Notre Dame asks one of Abelard's star pupils whether or not the master's latest treatise on the Trinity was heretical. "Of course it is heretical. Every book that ever was written about the Trinity is heretical, barring the Athanasian Creed. And even that one saves itself by contradicting everything it says as fast as it says it." We make bold to say what language is impoverished to express because, as Augustine pointed out in a famous passage, a worse alternative would be silence.

The best melodies to break the silence have been those which help us through metaphor to discover the truth of the Trinity in our own experience. What makes Augustine so profound a theologian, even to today's mind, is his creative use of metaphors, especially for the Trinity, thirteen of which can be found in *De Trinitate* alone. The Trinity comes alive in my faith when I think of the three faces of God (drawing from Schleiermacher's threefold revelation of God—in the world, in Christ, and in the church). Thus the one God relates to and can be seen in the world in three ways: the creative face of God, the human face of God, and the social face of God. The creative face of God is the divine activity in creation. The human face of God is the divine activity in Jesus Christ. The social face of God is the divine activity in community.

All analogies are hobbled by various handicaps. The problem with metaphors such as ice, liquid, and steam; sun, ray, and light (Tertullian); "Revealer-Revelation-Revealed-ness" (Karl Barth); or "Creator-Liberator-Advocate" (Letty Russell) is that they don't show how the persons of the Trinity share the same essence or interact with one another. The problem with analogies of time and space such as "God in creation, God in history, and God in present tense" (G. Elton Trueblood) or "God everywhere and always, God there and then, God here and now" (David H. C. Read) is that they lack personality (hence the clinging attraction of Holy "Ghost," for while it conjures up images of haunting, at least it conveys personality). The psychological analogies, such as "Lover-Loved-Love" or "Memory-Understanding-Will" (Augustine); and "Love Originating-Love Responding-Love Uniting" (Aquinas)—analogies adopted in our time by Dorothy Sayers and Bernard Lonergan—were rendered suspect for Martin Luther because they presume a congruence between the inner essence of the soul and the divine essence, thus violating Luther's doctrine of sin.

No analogy will fit perfectly or even comfortably, because God alone is triune. The Trinity is too big to ever wrap our minds around. It is the ultimate metaphor. "Let us freely leave to God the knowledge of himself," John Calvin wrote in his *Institutes*. "For he alone is a competent witness for himself, being only known by himself." Or as a character in Graham Greene's play *The Potting Shed* (1957) exclaims, "I couldn't believe in a God so simple I could understand him." But without an earthen vessel we cannot draw living waters from the deep wells of truth.

A third reason for the absence of trinitarian faith today lies in our short historical attention span and our dislike of tradition (the Count in Baldassar Castiglione's *The Book of the Courtier* [1528] speaks for many of us when he says, "If we will follow them of old time, we shall not follow them"). It has been modish to dismiss the Trinity as a pious riddle or an antique heirloom of little use or relevance that should be shelved along with other artifacts and memorabilia from the distant past. While we once brought the doctrine of the Trinity through the front door of our faith, we quickly hung it up in the hallway with all the other old coats we never wear but can't bring ourselves to throw out because of who gave them to us. We seldom take it along with us into the other rooms where we spend most of our time or outside in the cold where we need it most.

The tombstone of Governor William Bradford of Plymouth Plantation, who died in 1657, reminds us: "What our fathers with so much difficulty secured, do not basely relinquish." The authority of antiquity, as G. K. Chesterton was fond of saying, is a means of extending the franchise, and the vote of the past as well as the voice of our own spiritual consciousness continues to authenticate the mystery of an experience of God in three ways. Those who have jettisoned the doctrine of the Trinity in the interest of making theology more appealing to moderns have ruefully come to echo the reflection of Oxford chaplain Ronald Knox: "Dogmas may fly out at the window but congregations do not come in at the door." One of the most dynamic developments in recent theology has been the pushing of the Trinity to the center of the Christian life by pentecostalism and process theology.

Finally, our language about the Trinity tends to spin conceits, weave confusion, and be more complex than any language has the right to be. Just as there is nothing more humorous than philosophers trying to define humor, so there is nothing more confusing than theologians trying to clear up the confusions of the Trinity.

The *filioque* clause has divided Christianity into East and West for over one thousand years. The back-door insertion of the word *filioque* (Latin: "and from the Son") in the Nicene Creed more than two hundred years after the creed reached its final formulation in 381 is presently being reexamined by some religious groups, although its removal from a creed (in which it doesn't belong) is a different issue to theologians from its removal from theology (where it hasn't made much of a difference). Eastern theologians, more attuned to the "three in one" part of the paradox and especially to all that relates to the third member of the Trinity, have lectured loud and long that the dual procession of the Holy Spirit from the Father and the Son has given rise to a host of errors which subordinate the Spirit to the Son or the church and transform the body of Christ into a legalism of creed, canon, and office. Western theologians, predisposed to accent the "one in three" side to the paradox and particularly all that relates to the second member of the Trinity, have argued with equal shrillness that the procession of the Spirit from the Father through the Son leads to an unhealthy mysticism, and that it fails to provide adequate checks on the Spirit because it does not bind intimately enough the Word and the Spirit. Yet any reading of Augustine's definitive treatment of *filioque* theology reveals that the West is less far afield from the East than is commonly thought. The dispute over dual procession was whipped into a frenzy more by political than theological considerations, and the differences between Western Christians and Eastern Orthodox churches have always been more cultural than anything else.

Unlike the people of Alexandria and Constantinople, we are not moved to tears by preaching on the significance of *homoousios* (the Father and the Son are of the same essence) or *perichoresis* (Jesus' divine and human natures mutually inhere), by phrases such as "one in substance, but three in subsistence," by creeds like the Athanasian, which revels in paradox. Unlike the people of Rome and Byzantium, we are not moved to schism by sermons lifting up the Holy Spirit as "sent by both, begotten by neither." Formulas of the Trinity come and go, but the truth of our experience of a God who speaks to us in three voices— silence, monologue, and dialogue—remains the same from generation to generation. It is debates that limit how God speaks to us, such as the one about *filioque,* perpetuated long after it has ceased to have meaning to the life of faith, which give theology a bad name. The whole controversy over *filioque* ought to be retired to a theological rest home. There are more interesting things to fight about.

Joseph A. Bracken tells us where the exictement is in his book *What Are They Saying About the Trinity?* (1979). He isolates three bees in theologians' bonnets that are stirring up lively new insights about the faith and stinging us to a partial, sometimes painful awareness of the importance of the Trinity to contemporary Christian belief and behavior. What does our experience of God as Trinity tell us about the God of our experience? First, God exists as community; second, God suffers with community; and third, part of God's nature as community is feminine.

Aristotle once said that whoever has no need of society is either a beast or a god. Our knowledge today of the animal kingdom and the divine community would force Aristotle to search for other candidates. The social doctrine of the Trinity, first expounded by Richard of St.-Victor and elaborated by some nineteenth-century theologians, rejects the name for God many mystics have relished (THE ALONE) and replaces it with a conception of God as "Interpersonal Process" or, more intelligibly, as "Community." The social doctrine of the Trinity may be expressed as a syllogism: God exists in community; we are created in God's image; therefore we exist in community. The individuality of a lone "I" without another "I" curves in upon itself, sinking within itself from its own weight, robbed of reality. Before the world was created—the community model says—God was not alone, but existed in a community of three coequal persons.

Thus when God said, "It is not good that man should be alone," he knew whereof he spoke, for God was not alone either. The classic affirmation of "Trinity in unity and unity in Trinity" becomes rendered "Community in unity and unity in community." The Holy Spirit is the love that binds the divine community and the human community together; the power of cohesion, reconciliation, and love that draws unity from plurality. This symbol of the Trinity suggests variety and diversity within the Godhead at the same time that it expresses unity as family and society. The danger of the community model of the Trinity is that it suggests a mental picture of a divine nuclear family or a committee of three. When the center of gravity in the Godhead shifts from tri-unity to that of community, a fall into tritheism is made easier. Trinitarianism stays standing when the divine community is understood as a differentiated unity.

Christian theology has always asked the question: "What is God?" In one form or another the Christian tradition has always answered: "God is relationship; God is community; God is love." The symbol of God as community reinforces the social cast to human existence and reminds us that the fundamental pattern of human life is not one of independence and self-sufficiency but one of interdependence, reciprocity, mutuality, and self-emptying. As the Holy Spirit unites us to one another and to God, enabling the divine family to become our family, we find in the divine life a basis for the Christian life that is rich and deep in reconciliation and self-giving love.

There is an ancient philosophical technique that would have us try on the opposite of a truth with which we are struggling to see if it fits any better. When we try believing in unitarianism, do we discover with Abelard that the Trinity is "a necessary idea of reason"? What do we give up when we adopt nontrinitarian explanations of God? Right away we lose the paradox, mystery, and complexity of trinitarian theology for more simple, less majestic and satisfying ways of thinking. But most of all, writes Brian Hebblethwaite, "the conviction that God is love is the major casualty of unitarian theism." Trinitarian belief is intrinsically relational, thus pointing to a God whose core of being is a love that must find expression in community. The fullness of human life and the richness of God's own personal existence are not conveyed when we think in terms of one, or two, but only when we think of three. Perhaps this is why the concept of Trinity is not an exclusively Christian idea, but one that is common to many religious traditions in varying degrees (e.g., Gen. 1:26— "Let us make man in *our* image, after *our* likeness") and indeed, as Carl Jung has argued, one that is "an archetypal reality in human consciousness."

The second new development that focuses attention on the Trinity is the rediscovery of the ancient belief in Patripassianism (the third-century doctrine that the Father suffered through the Son). University of Chicago theologian

Gerald Birney Smith proved a reliable weathervane of shifting theological winds when he wrote back in 1909: "A suffering God, bearing the burden of evil in his world—this must be the conception of the coming theology." The belief that God could not lower himself to levels of human experience such as pain and suffering, a doctrine called the impassibility of God ("the most questionable aspect of classical theism" according to some theologians) is now widely discredited.

For most of Christian history, theologians have applied the stencils of Greek philosophy to the doctrine of the Spirit. They have spoken of the "apathy" of God using the original meaning of the word "apathy"—freedom from suffering and pain, beyond change and imperfection. But throughout the Christian tradition there have been dissenting voices, especially artists, poets, musicians, and the common folk, who have found grace sufficient in the heart-wrenching, mind-boggling mystery that there is "Another's Sorrow" (William Blake); that we are not alone in our suffering; that at the center of all reality is a Spirit that groaneth with our spirit, a God who is continually touched by our anguish, bruised by our iniquities, and tortured with our inhumanity.

It has always been God suffering that those unblessed with the awareness of theological subtleties have seen on the cross. In William Langland's *Piers Plowman* (ca. 1362) the answer to the question, "Who suffereth more than God?" is emphatic: "No person, I believe." In the fourteenth century, Albigensian Christians from an obscure village in southern France called Montaillou, whose testimonies before the Inquisition have been exhumed by the historian Emmanuel Le Roy Ladurie, told their interrogators that the pain of being burned at the stake was bearable because "God takes the pain upon himself." It is storied of the sixteenth-century painter Matthias Grünewald that he trudged to the plague-infested Vosges mountains and was so moved by the sight and sound of the incredible suffering there that he painted for those afflicted with the hideous "St. Anthony's fire" the *Crucifixion* that hangs in Colmar today, showing Christ's body twisted in torment as their bodies were deformed by the disease, Christ's limbs swollen as theirs were swollen in green and gangrenous agony. The hermits who lived in the mountains became ministering angels to these sufferers and during their last hours set them down where they could gaze on the picture. As the plague leeched out the last drops of life from their tangled bodies, they found strength and courage and maybe even joy from a painting that traced Calvary to the tears of God.

Recent literary expressions that correspond to artistic conceptions of a suffering divinity such as Grünewald's *Crucifixion* include Edwin Markham's poem "The Nail-Torn God," Simone Weil's *Waiting for God* (1951), and Graham Greene's play *The Living Room* (1953). Isaac Bashevis Singer, in "A Personal Concept of Religion," wrote: "God, the Creator, is Himself the universal Sufferer. Our suffering is His suffering. We are He." Jürgen Moltmann properly stands at the head of a long and growing procession of theologians including Dietrich Bonhoeffer, Kazoh Kitamori, Jacques Ellul, Frances Young, and others who have seen that the cross is part of the history of the Holy Trinity, that God himself is a victim of our violence, and that to believe in a God whose love is compromised by his perfection in a world of Dachaus, Dresdens, Nagasakis, and Cambodias is too much to ask. The Spirit of that same God who endured the cross, despising the shame, overcoming evil with suffering, is the same Spirit that can fill us with the patience that can make suffering our teacher and not our undertaker.

Yet, God has not bent over so far backward toward our humanity that he topples over into our finitude of muck and misery and is unable to get out. This is what has happened to the God of some process theologians. When God becomes as dependent on us as we are on him, the chronology of creation is rewritten: in the beginning was the world, and the world created God in its own image and processes. Similarly, we need to be careful to affirm the suffering of God and the perfection of God at the same time. The only God who can help us is a God who suffers with us. But a

God whose own being is held in the grip of human travail is a God who cannot help himself, much less us. For all his dancing on a tightrope in *The Crucified God* (1974), the logical conclusion of Moltmann's reasoning is that God died with Jesus on the cross. And if God died, then so too did our hope of resurrection. Those who push God's involvement in human suffering too far, Père Jean Galot has correctly observed, undercut their own position, for "the mysterious greatness of this suffering comes from the fact that it is the suffering of God: if it were not the suffering of an impassible God it would lose its own value."

The third and most controversial trend in trinitarian speculation is the use of feminine imagery for God and, most often, for the Holy Spirit. There is a confusion of genders for Spirit in the Bible. The Greek word *parakletos* is masculine; the Greek word *pneuma* (from which we get "pneumatic" drills, tires, balloons, etc.) is neuter; and the Hebrew word *ruach* is feminine (Syriac and Aramaic words for "spirit" are also feminine). The Bible thus warrants a multiple choice of images for the Holy Spirit: he, she, or it. Which should we choose?

In striking contrast to the world's other religious traditions, Christianity (along with Judaism and Islam) has overwhelmingly used "he" in speaking of God, although utopian movements with ties to Christianity have often believed that if "man" were created in the image of God ("male and female he created them"—Gen. 1:27), then God must be both male and female. Mystical theologians like Jakob Boehme and Emanuel Swedenborg, Shaker founder Mother Ann Lee, Johann Conrad Beissel of the Ephrata Cloister, Mary Baker Eddy of Christian Science, even the Mormons and the Moonies, all have prayed in some fashion to a "Father-Mother God." Yet the bulk of classic Christian doctrine teaches that God is beyond sexual categories, and at the same time Christian training in church and home teaches us very early to think of God as male. A little girl named Jennifer decided to write a letter to God. "Dear God," she began, "are boys better than girls? I know you are one but please try to be fair." This masculine image of

God is increasingly being called into question for biblical, historical, theological, and psychological reasons.

The Christian tradition and its Near Eastern setting where cults worshiping female goddesses were common are presently subject to extensive exploration by scholars such as Joan Chamberlain Engelsman, who has sought to find out what happened to "the feminine dimension of the divine," in her book of that title (1979). The results are fascinating and foreboding. Engelsman finds, for example, that the Jewish tradition of sophiology helped shape early christology, and that "the doctrine of the Trinity ultimately owes a great deal to the original desire of human beings to image God as both male and female." In the apocryphal Gospel According to Hebrews and The Acts of Thomas, and indeed in most of the Gnostic gospels unearthed and painstakingly researched by Elaine H. Pagels, the Holy Spirit is envisioned as the maternal element of the Trinity.

Hippolytus traced the Trinity in the Old Testament by allegorizing the story of Isaac, Jacob, and Rebekah into a type of the Holy Spirit. In Proverbs and John, the divine Wisdom *(Sophia)* or Word *(Logos)* is conceived of in archetypically feminine terms (see, for example, Prov. 8:22–31 and John 1:2–3). More familiar are the dove and the fire, both feminine symbols, and the likening of the church to a mother, as the bearer of the Spirit. The psychology that tells us that personal wholeness consists of a contrasexual harmony and balance between the feminine dimension in man and the masculine dimension in woman, necessitating an interior marriage between the masculine and feminine inside us, seems more and more substantiated the more we know about the Bible, history, and theology. Just as it is important for men to get in touch with their femininity, and for women to get in touch with their masculinity, so, the argument runs, it is important for Christians to get in touch with the masculine and feminine dimension of the divine community.

How can this be done? The most popular approach today, and one claimed by recent theories of marriage counseling, is to see the Holy Spirit as the feminine expression of God.

The problem with this solution is threefold: (1) it is without consistent biblical foundation; (2) its suggestion that the Trinity is a community of two males and one female not only fails to remedy the "bad masculine," as New Testament scholar Paul K. Jewett points out, but even makes it worse by entrenching masculine primacy in God's very being; (3) the Holy Spirit as the female principle of the Godhead unties the knot that unites the Holy Spirit to the Spirit of Christ.

A second proposal, made initially by Carl Jung, is more radical and more prone to scratch Protestant sensibilities. Jung suggests that we need, not a Trinity, but a Quaternity—Father-Son-Spirit-Virgin Mary. It is an idea whose time will never come.

A third alternative—and one that I find most congenial—is, not to locate the femininity of God in one or a new member of the Trinity, but to stress, as the early church "father" Clement of Alexandria was known to do, the presence of the feminine throughout the Trinity. While God ultimately transcends all sexual distinctions and indeed all images whatsoever, if the Bible can compare God to a father who cries over his wayward children (Jer. 3:4) and to a mother whose comfort never ceases (Isa. 66:13), why can't we? If Jesus can liken God in Luke 15 to a rejoicing shepherd (vs. 4–7), a waiting father (vs. 11–24), and a searching housewife (vs. 8–10), why can't we? If there is room for a great variety of images when we talk about God, including the "Motherhood of God," why should we curl our lips at the "Fatherhood of God?" Sometimes we should refer to God as "he"; other times as "she."

But we should never refer to God, or to the Holy Spirit, as "it." For the Holy Spirit is more than a cosmic power, divine principle, moral energy, or impersonal force. The Holy Spirit is either a being with personality or a metaphor. You can't speak as the Bible does of the Spirit of God having love, mind, emotions, understanding, wisdom, will, and holiness without implying something intensely personal. The problem is that "personality" suggests body, shape, and form, and the Holy Spirit is a "spirit." Yet the Holy

Spirit has distinctiveness, character, and personality, making any impersonal designations dangerously misleading. Any retreat from the relational language inherent in the "person" of the Holy Spirit (do you find either Karl Barth's proposed alternative "mode of being," or Karl Rahner's suggested "distinct manner of subsistence" better substitutes?) leads to standoffish, frosty, sterile images of God without power and without appeal.

3
THE HOME
OF THE SPIRIT

"Church" is a strange word. To the ear it sounds rounded, lurching out of the mouth like an unhappy burp that will not be kept down but must be kept quiet. To the eye it appears bounded, its beginning and ending stiff, imposing letters that seem to be doing all they can to squeeze the life out of a lonely vowel. When you say it slowly, the word is very cold, bland, and boring, almost dead—which is how many people experience church. Yet few things please God less than a lifeless "church." For the church is the place where we bump into God and rub elbows with each other. The church is the place where this world and the other meet. The church is, quite simply, the magical universe of the Spirit.

I shall never forget the excitement of returning after many years' absence to my hometown church. Here in its Sunday school rooms I had been anointed in the Christian tradition; in its sanctuary I had learned how to live through the fiery furnace of growing up, the lion's den of peer pressure, and the whale's belly of loneliness; in its choir loft I had been brought to ponder why Pentecostals should get all the good tunes; behind its organ I had discovered the joy of service; in its recreation hall I had undergone, along with most of the rest of the youth fellowship, a not-too-decent adolescent rebellion; in its bell tower I had kissed my first real girl friend; in its pastor's office I had risked talking about my call to the ministry; in its pulpit I had officiated and preached at my first funeral—my father's; in its community I had experienced the sparkle of the Spirit's presence.

Although the building was the same, my homecoming had taken me to a different church. This church was lifeless, corpse-cold, and—in the words of a character from Walker Percy's *A Second Coming* (1980)—had the smell of death in it. If attendance figures mean anything, the church counted more people among the dead than among the living. The pastor, who had settled in for a long life's nap, spoke as if the church were a casket for the eternal. In spite of a few unsquashable souls whose warmth radiated their belief in the power of the resurrection, the congregation's sagging spirits pulled down every hymn and response. It is not true that "you can't kill a church," for here was a church whose death would have been no different from its life. It is said that H. L. Mencken, when informed that Calvin Coolidge was dead, responded, "How can they tell?" There must be a special place in eternity reserved for those who become party to making this word "church" an epitaph on the living.

I looked around at the handful of glassy-eyed youths, whose sole inspiration was coming from the stained-glass windows. Sunday morning worship had come to mean for them the most painful hour of the week. I thought how different I might have been if I had not learned to TGIS (Thank God It's Sunday), if I had come to associate the church solely with "bingo, bazaars, and bad sermons," if the last place I had come to expect fun and fire was in the church. Tom Marshfield, in John Updike's *A Month of Sundays* (1975), came to mind. Reflecting on his youth, he said: "Churches bore for me the same relation to God that billboards did to coca-cola; they promoted thirst without quenching it." During the sermon I began to yearn even for billboards.

As a historian who is not unaccustomed to the odor of rotted religion and rancid piety, I could cerebrally remind myself that the perversion of the best yields the worst. But viscerally I angrily identified with Voltaire's outlook on the church, *Écrasez l'infâme* ("Crush the vile thing"), and felt an unholy kinship with the California churchgoer who recently, after sitting through a boring service until he could take no more, was arrested and charged with attacking the priest in the middle of his sermon. "God made me do it," he told the police as they led him away.

What had happened to my hometown church? One is tempted, though one would be wrong, to say that the Holy Spirit had taken upward flight and settled elsewhere. Yet it is not the Holy Spirit who passes us by; it is we who pass her by. It is we who have failed to be formed by the Bible, which knows no other kind of church but a pentecostal church, no other kind of believer than a charismatic believer. The gospel may be preached, and the sacraments administered, but unless the Easter Son comes alive through the Pentecost Spirit and is allowed to work in a community, unless personal gifts and graces are articulated, activated, and celebrated, our efforts yield little more than the hallowing of hollowness at worst or ho-hum spirits at best. In my hometown church the Holy Spirit had become a slumbering seed, underground, unwatered, unknown. "Surely the Lord was in this place; and we knew it not."

"How is the Holy Spirit related to the church?" is a question that is raised every time we recite "I believe in the Holy Spirit, the holy catholic church ..." A favorite answer of a large portion of the Christian community has been to say that Jesus gave the Holy Spirit to the church, thus comparing the church to the ark of Noah outside of which there is no place to be saved from the flood of judgment. Whatever answer we give to this question will be crucial, for it will determine much of how we experience the Spirit and how we shape our lives. All traditions believe that the Holy Spirit is present in the church in some way. Where traditions differ is on the question of how the Spirit got there. Some say Jesus gave the Holy Spirit to the church (whether understood as a spiritual or a juridical entity), and others say Jesus gave the Holy Spirit to persons. The question everyone is addressing, however, is whether the Holy Spirit is something we possess, or something that possesses us.

We saw in the last chapter how the churches in East and West have disagreed as to whether the Holy Spirit proceeds from the Father through the Son, or from both the Father and the Son. But both agree that the Holy Spirit proceeds. To where? To whom is the Holy Spirit given? Is the primary work of the Holy Spirit to build up the believer, as John's Gospel would have it, or to build up the church, as Paul's letters would suggest? Is the locus for the activity of the Holy Spirit in the church or in the person? Does the Holy Spirit make her home in our body, or in the body of Christ? Does the church enjoy the Spirit because the Holy Spirit first dwells in the hearts of the church's members, or do persons enjoy the Spirit to the extent that they come under the umbrella of the church where the Holy Spirit dwells? A new dimension has been added to this debate by process theologians, who have revived the patristic resistance (Origen excepted) to the institutionalizing or individualizing of the Spirit. Can the range of the Spirit's operation, they contend, be restricted to the church, or to the person? Doesn't it encompass the world? The tendency of the Roman church has been to hold the Holy Spirit hostage to the offices of the church; the tendency of Protestantism has been to make the Holy Spirit captive to the individual, either through binding the Spirit to the Word or by locating the Spirit's home in the hearts of the faithful.

The great theologian of the Spirit, the apostle Paul, sends mixed signals. There are two passages in which he speaks of the body as a temple of the Holy Spirit (I Cor. 3:16–17 and I Cor. 6:19–20). In the former he is referring to the church and in the latter he is referring to the individual. Those who have followed the path illuminated by the former sometimes talk as if the dove of the Spirit were only a bird caged in a Gothic cathedral, there being no salvation possible outside the edifice. (Cyprian is the third-century theologian most famous for posting apostolic bouncers at the Pearly Gates: "He cannot have God as his father who has not the church as his mother.") Those who have been guided by the latter (one denomination talks of the human heart as a three-tiered throne on which sit the three persons of the Trinity) often exhibit the extreme individualism we have come to associate with various forms of Protestantism, where the church is little more than aggregations of individuals, each person functioning as his or her own little church or temple of the Spirit. Martin Luther, who warned about the difficulty of this conception in screening self-spirits from the Holy Spirit, got into a shouting match with certain disciples of Thomas Münzer over this "Spirit made me do it" behavior, accusing them of "having swallowed the Holy Ghost, feathers and all." Münzer retorted that without the Holy Spirit, God was not real no matter if Luther "devoured a hundred thousand Bibles." Luther's solution to the problem of the enthusiasts was to chain the Spirit to the literal word. The Roman solution before him had been to bind the Spirit to the church's ministry and tradition. Both sides were right in trying to establish tests and checks of the Spirit; both sides were wrong in trying to "bind" and control the Spirit.

What we need is a new formulation of the question, "To whom was the Holy Spirit given at Pentecost?" To say that the Holy Spirit was given to persons is to say only more democratically what the Old Testament said. To say that the Holy Spirit was given to the church is to say that the Holy Spirit was given to something before that something existed. For is this not what the Holy Spirit did at Pentecost—and what the Spirit did not do at any other time—namely, create a new community? Jesus bequeathed to humanity not a book, or a theology, or a religion, but a community. Indeed, after the Holy Spirit came upon Jesus at his baptism, the first sermons he preached were on the coming kingdom of God (Matt. 4:17). The key purpose of the Pentecost event, wrote John Calvin, was the "gift of community." There was a new creation at Pentecost, a creation called *ekklesia* or church, the official name in Acts 5:11 for the *koinonia* or "fellowship" of the Spirit (II Cor. 13:14; Phil. 2:1).

The Holy Spirit is the God who creates community. And the issue of the Spirit and the Word, so critical to Protestantism, is resolved not by binding the Spirit to the Word but by placing the Word within the Spirit, or, in other words, insisting that the Scriptures be interpreted within the shared life of building community. The biblical drama begins, not with the virginal birth of the Big Bang, but with the Spirit of God brooding over darkness and creating order out of chaos. It ends with the Spirit of God breathing through the kingdom of a New Jerusalem. Between Genesis and the Apocalypse is the story of creation, the creation of saving communities by the Spirit of God.

The Holy Spirit is not experienced within the confines of an organization known as the church. Nor is it experienced merely within the context of the sacraments, fellowship, and discipline of a living organism known as the church. The life of Christ is more than an institutional or social life. It is a life that *builds* and *creates* social lives. The principal work of the Holy Spirit is not simply to bestow life on a community. More precisely, it is to bring a community to life. Like leaven added to dough, bringing a loaf to life, the Holy Spirit wants to permeate an environment until a glob of people, dense with selfish discord and heavy with small-mindedness, is transformed into something fresh, buoyant, and beautiful. For this reason, if we are to experience the fullness of the Spirit, we cannot experience it in ourselves alone, or by membership in a community and support of a community building, but only through personal participation in community-building.

Holy Spirit is not God within us. Holy Spirit is God between us. In the language of Martin Buber, "Spirit is not in the I but between I and Thou." It takes two to feel the Spirit, Matt. 18:20 reminds us, for "where two or three are gathered together in my name, there am I in the midst of them." Holy Spirit is a "midst" God, and the Christian life is not a personal journey toward self-discovery or self-fulfillment but a social quest. But, you say, what about the extreme cases, people on the fringe of faith—the traveler stranded on a deserted island, the monk in a cloister, the hermit in a cave? How can the Holy Spirit be the God who builds community and still be at work in their lives? For the handful who live, not on the mainland where almost all of us spend our lives, but on deserted islands, the community is present and growing through the power of memory and imagination, just as real and binding as the lingering love for deceased or distant family and friends. For the monk or hermit, the community is present and growing through the power of tradition and prayer. Like the traveler, monk, or hermit, there is much that we do apart from other people. When we pray, for example, we often shut the door—the door to distraction, but not the door to people. For even when we pray in the solitude of our rooms, we experience the presence of the Holy Spirit because we take the concerns of the community there with us.

I live less than three miles from the Abbey of the Genesee, a Trappist monastery made famous by Henri Nouwen. Each year as one of their awareness trips the church confirmation class attends evening vespers at the Abbey. Before we enter the dark stone sanctuary the class listens as Brother Anthony explains to them how monks love the world just as Jesus loved the world, and that the monastic tradition of separation from the world can actually be a means toward a heightened identification with the world. Keeping alive the memory of the past, Brother Anthony says as he describes the community of tradition of which he is a part, can actually be a means of keeping alive the voice of the future. The words ring true when, after the bells have summoned us for evening vespers, individual monks break their silence with prayers of intercession for world leaders, current events, local political conditions, and even the church confirmation class. Many a night at 2 A.M. I have laid a weary head on the pillow and found deep peace in the knowledge that when the rest of the Genesee Valley was falling asleep, some monks were rising to begin another day and keep the lamp of prayer burning.

The Holy Spirit weaves us all together, both island and mainland persons, into a tapestry of relationships known as the church. The importance of this stitching to the New Testament is revealed in its abundance of "syn" words, pointing to the social, communal, corporate dimension of our faith existence. "Faith and community are inextricably joined together," Robert McAfee Brown has written. "Community can only be created around a faith; faith can only be creative within a community." There is a difference, worth paying attention to, between the contemporary trend back to the days when authority was located in the organic community rather than the morally instructed individual, and the call of the gospel to find the life of the Spirit in the creation of community. The Puritans had a way of putting this epigrammatically: "The sparks are beaten forth by the flints striking together." The sparks of the Spirit's presence and power fly upward in the "midst" of flinty souls and shattered selves touching one another, building one another up, and reaching out together toward wholeness and community.

What this all means is that it takes two to make a Christian. The only way to God is through other people. We don't go to heaven by ourselves, but in company with our brothers and sisters. Or as one of my students likes to put it, we can only get to heaven in a crowd. Jesus called people into community, and the mission of the church is to do likewise. The purpose of salvation is to be saved in, to, and for community. The Greek word *sozo* means both "save" and "heal": to save is to bring back from a fractured state, to heal is to reconstitute community. If we define "salvation" as William Tyndale did in 1525 in his English translation of the Greek New Testament, using the word "health" to convey the concept we now know as "salvation" (meaning complete psychosomatic wholeness, mental, physical, and spiritual), there is no individual salvation, only a community of salvation. Just as God exists in community, so for our "health" we who bear the divine image need also to exist in community. Outside of community we are not God's image, but God's smudge.

I shall have long memories of an encounter with an American Indian college student who was undergoing severe emotional distress. Eventually the fact surfaced that his mother was Mohawk and his father Tonawanda Seneca. Among the Mohawks the lineage is traced through the father, and among the Tonawanda Seneca it is traced through the mother. Even though he was born a native American, he was born an orphan, for he had no tribe. Without a community, he felt totally alone and isolated. There can be nothing worse.

My eleven-year-old son came home from school one day and told about a creative writing class with a guest author who came to teach her craft. She gave the class the assignment to imagine that they were walking down a sandy beach one "gray, misty day" when suddenly they stumbled upon a cave with a door. Behind that door, she said, they would discover the thing they feared most in life. "Now finish the story." When my son handed me his account of opening the door to the cave, I knew what I would read—a story about being pawed apart by grisly monsters, or an interstellar tale about being swept out into outer space to orbit for eternity in nothingness. Here was his story:

> The door felt rusty, wet and very cold. It streaked up my spine like a sharp, cold knife piercing into my skin. Its wood was very rough and stunk like a skunk. I felt the urge to scream, but I didn't. I had a feeling of curiousness to open the door. I turned the clammy knob and opened the creaky door. Suddenly I was transported to a city—a city of death. For no one was there. Just parked cars and the wind thrashing against the trees. The thing I dreaded most had happened. No one to share my thoughts with, no one to express my depressions with, no one to talk to, no companion. Just loneliness.

I felt a lot older that week, for a little boy had become a man.

There is no more horrible wound in life, no greater killer, than isolation and loneliness. It is no accident that the likeliness of suicide is in proportion to either the liking of isolation or the degree of social withdrawal. Similarly, it is not surprising that psychiatry's success at healing has been less than spectacular, for psychoanalysis tends to absolutize the individual and to show little sensitivity to the social context of living. The physics of life tells a similar story, for even atoms apparently need to rub up against each other. The physical sciences teach us that in atomic society twelve is the "maximum coordination number," the maximum number of atoms that can be positioned around a central atom and still touch it, testifying to the enormous power of small groups in the universe of physical chemistry. Human society displays a parallel law of maximum coordination, but only gradually are we coming to appreciate the necessity and power of small groups for our psychological stability and spiritual well-being. Healers, both those in black robes and those in white coats, still most often treat a person in isolation and not in community, where a yoke is easy because a burden is shared.

The unrelated, self-sufficient individual is not a whole person, but a broken, alienated, sinful person. An Oriental story illustrates this understanding of sin. A man crying from the depths of hell is pleading for release. When asked the good he has done in his life, all he can remember is that, while walking in the woods one day, he saw a spider and did not kill it. At once the thin silvery thread of a spider web is let down to him in hell. Grasping eagerly at this rope of hope, he is slowly lifted out of his misery. His fellow sufferers, seeing him about to escape, clutch his garment and his feet. Amazingly, all begin to be lifted up together. But the man, fearing the web might break, starts kicking at them, crying "Let go! Let go!" When they do let go, the thread breaks, and all fall back into hell. The thread, strong enough for a community of sufferers, could not bear the heavy burden of a selfish soul. C. Norman Kraus puts this theology so very well in his *The Community of the Spirit* (1974): "To be saved means to be in authentic relationship with fellow humans under the lordship of Christ. Salvation means the restoration of community which the Old Testament prophets referred to as the 'peace of God,' and which Jesus referred to as the kingdom of God."

In this light the horrid, ugly phrase "Outside the church there is no salvation" is transformed into a beautiful and liberating thought for two reasons. First, as Ladislaus Boros points out, if we express the concept positively—"Where the church is, there is salvation"—this is equivalent to saying, "Where there is salvation, there is the church."

Wherever brokenness is giving way to wholeness, evil to good, lies to truth, oppression to justice, selfishness to service; wherever people and structures are being made whole, there is, however partial and fragmentary, the church, the formation of community. Secondly, C. P. Snow, Robert Heilbroner, Alexander Solzhenitsyn, Rustum Roy, and others are leading a parade of scientists and intellectuals who have rallied behind this banner long since discarded by Christians (*"Extra ecclesiam nulla salus"*) because they believe it is too late for any hope for humanity, any salvation for the world, outside of a religious framework. The word "religion" stems from the Latin word *religare*, which means to tie securely, to bind together. The only forces powerful enough to halt the lethal folly of our ways by binding us into bonds of trust and respect and sanity are religious forces.

But there is a second Latin word from which our understanding of the nature of "religion" derives. It is the word *religere*, which means to reflect deeply, to contemplate with awe. Whereas *religare* points to the social, *religere* points to the existential, mystical dimensions of life in the Spirit. One of the saints of the Middle Ages became so disturbed by the Christian preoccupation with the hereafter, to the detriment of experiencing life with God in the here and now, that he wrote the lullaby to life, "All the way to heaven is heaven."

As we experience union with God in the moments life brings us, or more precisely, the moments we bring to life, the way to heaven can be heaven. This is why everyone who lives a life of the Spirit is something of a mystic, for everyone who builds community experiences the sacred and the divine presence. The Christian tradition obliquely acknowledges this when it defines the church as "the mystical body of Christ," which, according to Thomas Aquinas, "includes potentially all human beings who have existed or will exist until the end of the world." The Holy Spirit is "inChristed"—to adopt an ancient phrase of the mystics—into a community; the Holy Spirit is the breath of God in the soul of the church, the mystical body of Christ.

Christ is the head, the community is the body, but the Spirit is the soul.

Philosophers tell us that the essence of the human soul is the capacity for self-transcendence, the experience that one exists and the experience that one experiences that one exists, and on and on. Similarly, the essence of the church's soul is the capacity to experience the Spirit of God as Holy and as Spirit. God may be in everything, and everything may be in God; but God who is everywhere in general, scrambled into life and mixed into everything, is a God who is nowhere in particular and a God we cannot consciously know. In the words of the tenth-century theologian St. Simeon: "It is not enough that we have received the Holy Spirit. We must be consciously aware of it." The church is the place where the Holy Spirit is distinctively present and known as Spirit and "intensively active" as Holy—building and conforming the body to the mind of Christ. If "history is the 'sacrament' of Christian ethics," as Jürgen Moltmann has argued, the church is the sacrament of Christian experience. It is the sacred space where God is peculiarly present in personality and in power.

How dearly we need this dimension of social mysticism. It is not as if we were unfamiliar with mysticism altogether, for the mysticism of the human is alive and well. Former basketball star Bill Russell talks about the "mystical" moments of sports, the peak experiences or "sweet spots in time" when the spectacular appears routine, when a nonchalant Julius Erving can make his gravity-defying way through a minefield of limbs and, with rifles for legs, shoot up to the rafters and drill the ball into the basket. What is, after all, the *Guinness Book of World Records* but a catalog of mystical experiences? Humans work in mysterious ways—it announces on every page—their miracles to perform.

But the mysticism of the human is exactly the opposite from the mysticism of the divine. The mysticism of the human is to write one thousand musical pieces in thirty years and thus to be the fastest composer who ever lived. The mysticism of the divine is to realize that Mozart made all that music out of twelve notes and noises. The mysticism of the divine is not the spectacular made routine, but the routine made spectacular, the commonplace uncommon, the experience of the extra in the ordinary, bursts of transcendence in the "midst" of the everyday. Flannery O'Connor knocked herself out book after book teaching us this—there is the sacred to be found in the ordinary, the supernatural in the natural. There is another world in this one. Heaven is planted deep into the soil of earth, and it breaks out in the most unexpected places.

The problem is, we live in a society that has been swept clean of transcendence; where the sacred has been secularized, and the secular (television, sports, etc.) sacralized; where third-person experiences have replaced first-person experiences; where reflected forms of religious conviction, a sort of moonlight piety, illumine our darkness. There are at least two reasons why this is so.

First, we have been chloroformed by comfort to the point where we are numb to the wonder and worth of the simple. "The tree which moves some to tears of joy," William Blake once wrote, "is in the eyes of others only a green thing that stands in the way." One of life's big paradoxes is that the things of this world that are scarcest—gold, silver, jewels— are most worthless, while the things that are most common—trees, water, air, light, people—are the most valuable.

Second, it is difficult to have a religious experience today, even when you go to church, because Western theology has vacuumed up the more mystical, serendipitous experiences from the floor of faith and covered it with the carpet of doctrine. We have been more interested in the capacity of language to comprehend the divine than in the capacity of people to experience the divine. If there is to be a genuine spirituality in today's world, it will need to come through the rediscovery of social mysticism.

Many who have defined "mysticism"—and such scholarly attempts constitute a thriving cottage industry—have taken the straight and narrow path to the hermit's cave and the monastic cell where lonely, tormented souls embark on inward journeys and find immodest union with the divine in visions and voices, trances and meditations. The wider road, which in some contexts is said to lead to destruction, in this case actually leads to discovery. There can be no rigid, tight definition of mysticism, and if there were such a definition, no one could use it. Thomas Aquinas, who was probably the last person in history to know everything there was to know, defined it better than anyone: mysticism is "the knowledge of God through experience."

Mysticism is the tracking of transcendence, the sniffing out of the beyond, until God becomes real, present, here for you. Mysticism says that we must partake of the divine to know the divine. Social mysticism says that the divine is to be experienced through building community. Perhaps better than anyone else, Teilhard de Chardin has seen that mysticism is a journey of "centering"—of passing by a self-centered existence, passing through an existence centered in self, and finding existence centered in the Spirit where the inner and the outer are integrated, action and contemplation balanced, and personhood and community blended. Social mysticism is not an altered state of consciousness or a solitary quest for an encounter with God, but a heightened consciousness of, and a "sober intoxication" (Philo of Alexandria) with, God's encounter with the world.

The church is the home of mystics because the church attempts to bridge the chasm between the divine and the human. Mysticism reconciles transcendence with immanence, maintaining them in proper proportion. The problem with a totally transcendent God who is absolutely other is that God is too cold and too remote. The problem with a totally immanent God who inhabits and informs the world is that God is too shallow, too intimate with culture. Our experience of the Holy Spirit makes the transcendent immanent. The God who is beyond us becomes the God who is among us. That familiar distinction, a darling of theologians, between the "numinous," or the awareness of the holy, and the "mystical," or the merging with divine reality, collapses in a fundamental similarity: the experience of the transcendent as immanent.

John Wesley drew from Eastern spirituality, Counter-Reformation mysticism, German pietism, and Romans 8 to express all this in his very mystical notion of the "witness of the Spirit," where every believer is granted an inward assurance and testimony of the Spirit. Because this witness sometimes comes through contemplation, some have defined mysticism exclusively in terms of the contemplative life. To do this is to confuse means with ends. The end of corporate mysticism is the experience of the life of God in the soul of community. Whenever you have been loved beyond your lovability, you have had a mystical experience; whenever you have been forgiven beyond your hope, the Holy Spirit has witnessed with your spirit; whenever you forget God, and God does not forget you, you have been engulfed in the mystical.

I can think of little that is sadder than to live in the Spirit without recognizing it. So often we suffer from what Kierkegaard called "shutupness"—we close ourselves to the occasions when ordinary moments are charged with joy and electrified with ecstasy. Mysticism is the transformation of the everyday world into an imaginative universe. Social mysticism is the holy made available, the Spirit made known, in community. In mystery the Spirit is experienced, in faith embraced. "A mystery is something in which I am myself involved," Gabriel Marcel writes. Social mysticism is getting caught up in the mysteries of life: hearing the Holy Spirit speak to us of the mystery of life which we ultimately call God, and of the mystery that took bodily form, Jesus Christ. Social mysticism is the experience of the transcendent God, immanent in love and power, in communion with us.

Social mysticism is not a skylight to heaven but a window to planet earth, not an escape into a womb but engagement in the world. Modern studies of desert monasticism increasingly emphasize its connection with social conscience, action, and protest. Anthropological studies of ritual such as those done by Anthony F. C. Wallace point to the mystical elements in community rituals that serve as a preparatory activity for full-throttle engagement. Religion begins in mysticism (a "domestic experience"); but as liberation theologians remind us, it ends in politics (a "foreign policy"). Or as Jonathan Edwards would have put it, we are never saved for our own benefit.

Donald G. Miller tells the story of a Ph.D. student who embarked on a study of the Holy Spirit in the New Testament. He confessed that, to his great surprise, at the end of his journey he had discovered the church. So have we.

4
THE LANGUAGE
OF THE SPIRIT

Holy Spirit is God building community. Will any community do? Is God fussy about what kind of community he builds? Or is the Holy Spirit indifferent to the content of community so long as the Humpty Dumpty of the human race is put back together again, whether it be by Mother Teresa or Jim Jones, Abraham Lincoln or Adolf Hitler? To ask the question this way is to answer it. Clearly, it does make a difference what kind of community the Holy Spirit forms.

So how does a Spirit-filled community act, and what does it look like? A community shapes itself by reference to the past, necessitating a glance backward into church history. There is an old law of the woods that says a stream of water is purest at its source. To discover the kind of pentecostal downpours that showered the early church and are refreshing churches today we need to go back to Acts, the first church history textbook, and to read in chapter 2 what the first Christian church looked and acted like. It is disquieting to discover that the first churches, such as those in Jerusalem and Corinth, were far from models of spirituality—a rebuke to my unsanctified disillusionment about my hometown church and a reminder that resurrection is one of the many surprises the Holy Spirit always has up her sleeves.

The first gift of the Holy Spirit to the church was tongues. Spirit-filled churches have the gift of tongues. There is a special language of the Spirit that the church must speak, a language identifiable and understandable by all because of its distinctive grammar, mood, accents, and idioms. There are various tongues spoken in churches today—educatese, scientese, churchese, bureaucratese—but the Spirit speech spoken by Augustine, Luther, Wesley, Edwards, Finney, and Rauschenbusch is to many an alien tongue. The Day of Pentecost launched a new language in the human vocabulary, a language with which the church is called to address the world.

The grammar of Spirit speech is, first of all, intelligent and informed. The early church sought instruction and learning, "they were continually devoting themselves to the apostles' teaching" (Acts 2:42). Early Christians had minds that were alive, not working mechanically but dynamically, and their faith was one that would, in Augustine's words, "believe in thinking and wish to think in believing." Jacob Neusner, one of America's foremost Judaic scholars, was invited to Brigham Young University to deliver a series of lectures on the essence of Judaism. He chose for his title a motto he had read on Brigham Young University's stationery: "The Glory of God Is Intelligence." Study, learning, scholarship are just as much acts of piety and devotion as prayer and praise. Indeed, there is an old rabbinic saying that an hour of study is in the eyes of God as an hour of prayer. It is not only on our knees that we shall grow tall, but also on our posteriors. Isaiah 11:2 and John 14:26 provided the Middle Ages in particular with text appeal for recognizing the Holy Spirit as the fount of knowledge. Medieval art pictured saints celebrated for their thinking and writing with a dove hovering by their head and breathing into their ear the wisdom of God.

Whenever knowledge increases, true religion is enhanced. Whenever the church is content to let inherited opinion dispense with continued inquiry and critical scholarship, the church's native tongue is garbled and mangled. "To call the new learning heresy," Erasmus wrote, "is to make orthodoxy synonymous with ignorance." We know the church as a worshiping community. We tend to forget that it is also a thinking community. A mindless faith dishonors, even blasphemes God. A woman critical of John Wesley's appetite for inquiry came to him one day and said, "Mr. Wesley, God can get along right well without your scholarship." He replied, "True, madam, and God can get along quite well without your ignorance." We may not be able to get into heaven headfirst, as an old Scottish evangelist used to say, but we cannot get in without our heads. A spirit-filled church's vocabulary will be an inspiration to the spirit, an invitation to the soul, and a challenge to the mind.

The mood of Spirit speech is, secondly, reconciling. This is part of the meaning of that word found in Acts 2:42, *koinonia*, which we translate as "fellowship" but which stems from the adjective *koinos*, which means "common." Pentecost created the first Christian fellowship where there was a spirit of common unity, witnessing to the Holy Spirit as the divine power that brings all things into harmony with God and with each other. Pentecost engineered the first global village since Eden. It was a day when cultural barriers were blasted and when relational bridges were built. The first tower of Babel fractured the family of humanity into many languages; the second tower of Babel reconciled the family of humanity through many languages. The Spirit doesn't mash us all into one mold. Instead of speaking one language we learn to understand others. The language of the Spirit unifies as it diversifies, and those theologians who would make Christ the source of unity in the church, and the Holy Spirit the source of diversity, forget that the Holy Spirit which creates, binds, and perfects community is the source of both—of reconciling diversity. In fact, the Holy Spirit promotes unity by preserving diversity, which halts a community's slide from unity into uniformity of method and unanimity of thought.

The Holy Spirit does not lead us to unanimity, because the Christian life is not a system of doctrine. The Holy Spirit does not lead us to uniformity, because the Christian life is not a system of management or worship. But the Holy Spirit does lead us to unity, because the Christian life is a system of community. Those who think the church must be sociologically homogeneous to grow listen more to the social sciences than to the Spirit. The early church, by the reckoning of many church growth experts, should not have grown because its membership was too pluralistic. The Holy Spirit's home is the one place where all people can feel at home, and this unity of the church rates so high with Luke and Paul that they warn anyone who encourages disunity, as Ananias and Sapphira did, of the penalty for desecrating the temple of God, namely, death (Acts 5:1–11; I Cor. 3:17).

Of course, where two or three are gathered together, there is Eris (the Greek goddess of discord) in the midst of them. Some idealists like Thomas K. Beecher, a member of the great nineteenth-century Beecher clan, have argued that conflict is fatal to fellowship, and have refused to tolerate it within the church. After being called to the Park Street Church in Elmira, New York, Beecher wrote to his new church and promised them that with the first sound of a church fight or bickering, "your pastor shall have taken his departure. I shall never be party to a church squabble anywhere or remain in a church where one exists." Yet we know from our reading of Acts that controversies and factions were common to early churches like those at Antioch and Corinth, that Paul feuded with Peter about the faith, and Barnabas quarreled with Paul. In any reconciliation there will be both oil and vinegar tossed in.

The mark of the Spirit's presence is not the quiet of agreement, even among Christians. It is, rather, the quality of argument and the constancy of reconciliation. "Confusion abounds," John Courtney Murray has well written; "genuine disagreement is hard to come by." Conflict that is genuine, creative, and peaceful is a sign of life and vigor, not the opposite.

Some of the most agreeable and irenic contacts I have ever had occurred in the waiting room of my doctor's office where I go to get all-too-frequent allergy shots. Though its occupants may be at loggerheads on almost any political or religious issue, the spirit in that waiting room is one of anonymous goodwill and friendliness. The only problem is that there is no real communication going on except chatty pleasantries, no true intersection of worlds. Where there are no squabbles, there is no community being built, and no divine Spirit present. If where the Holy Spirit is there is liberty and love and truth; if the Spirit makes us more alive, more authentic, more unique; if the Spirit transforms not I's into We's but I's into more distinctive I's, then there will also be different opinions and many points of view in the church, and even in eternity. I find it hard to picture Calvin and Wesley, Wagner and Debussy, Hans Küng and John Paul II, dwelling together in heaven without disagreement. Conflict is a function of our freedom, a sign that we who have been created in the likeness of the triune God are developing and deepening that image. The language of the Spirit seeks not to banish conflict, but to put back together shattered selves and bring back together broken-up, broken-off people. Spirit speech articulates the only vocabulary that can answer the great unresolved question of the human species: how to get along with one another.

The third distinctive feature of the church's Spirit speech is the language of passion, the speech of "gladness and singleness of heart" (Acts 2:46). To say that "the earth is the Lord's and the fulness thereof" is to say that the world is precious in God's sight and something about which we ought to care passionately. This is not the passion of the "can't change their minds and won't change the subject" fanatics whose chilling seriousness, like the blighting frost, destroys the fragile blossoms of joy. Nor is it the passion of today's romantics who reveal a yearning only for possessions. Nor is it the passion of the pragmatists like the nineteenth-century railroad workers in the American West whose motto of ruthless indomitability was: "I will find a way or I will make a way."

Rather, in speaking of the language of passion we mean the passion of "enthusiasm," which Louis Pasteur, in a speech before the French Academy, called one of the most beautiful words in the language because it means "God in us." It is the passion that comes from love in action, the Holy Spirit among us in wisdom and in power. Passion is the daring of Christ, who would eat with publicans and meet with prostitutes to demonstrate God's unsparing love. Passion is the single-mindedness of the paralytic's four friends, who risked their reputations and even their lives by lowering him through the roof so that he might come near the healing touch of Christ. Passion is the unconventional boldness of Martin Luther, who wrote in 1522 the following letter to the Elector Frederick of Saxony soliciting help for an aged and sick man named Christopher Pfaffenbeck:

> I fall at Your Grace's feet and humbly ask Your Grace to have pity on this poor man and support him in his old age. . . . God has more Schneebergs [the Elector's silver mine]. Your Grace's realm need not fear that it will be bankrupted by charity; it has never happened so before. . . . If the "give" is rich, the "and it shall be given to you" is far richer. . . . Your Grace may be assured that I will not leave this man in this condition, even if I have to go out and beg for him myself. And if that does no good, I shall even rob and steal the first thing I lay my hands on, especially if it belongs to the Elector of Saxony. So I ask Your Grace to hear this plea of mine, for my own sake, so that I may not have to go a-stealing. I would not enjoy it if Your Grace had to hang me for stealing.

Passion is the "spiritual equivalent of war," as the church follows its Lord in bringing to a world of evil and injustice and oppression not plowshares, but swords (Matt. 10:34).

Because Christians are too timid and polite to bring their faith to a boil, passion is cooled out of the church. It was not always so. Stephen F. Austin opposed allowing Protestant ministers into the fledgling Texas colony because they "would ruin us." One preacher "would do more mischief in this colony than a dozen horse thieves." How times have changed in the modern era of scarcity, where scarcest of all is the passion of our convictions. Yet when a child reaches out to touch a rattlesnake, we raise our voice a little. Why then, when God's children trample on the body of Christ and kick its face in, is there a reluctance to raise our voice a little? Only the passion of a raised voice can awaken a slumbering society to see that it is on a joyride to suicide. A muffled witness will not do; minced words will avail little. "Moonlight dries no mittens," Carl Sandburg has reminded us. You need the blazing heat of sunlight; you need fire. And a church professing to have been stoked by the Spirit ought to be fired up. The church will accomplish nothing great in this world without passion. The kingdom of God cometh not by halfheartedness.

A fourth characteristic of the church's language is its accent on compassion. The most profound question directed to an episcopal candidate from the United Methodist Northeastern Jurisdiction a few years ago was from a Boston woman who methodically asked each prospective bishop who appeared before her area delegation the same stunning question: "Who are the lepers?" Who are the lepers to whom the Spirit has led us, and how is the church feeding them? Henri Nouwen, who has picked up where Thomas Merton's later writing on compassion left off, tells an old Sufi story that says it all about the difference between a church without and a church with compassion.

Once upon a time, there was a man who strayed from his own country into a world known as the Land of Fools. He soon saw a number of people flying in terror from a field where they had been trying to reap wheat. "There is a monster in that field," they told him. He looked and saw that it was a watermelon.

He offered to kill the "monster" for them. When he had cut the melon from its stalk, he took a slice and began to eat it. The people became even more terrified of him than they had been of the melon. They drove him away with pitchforks crying, "he will kill us next, unless we get rid of him."

It so happened that at another time another man also strayed into the Land of Fools, and the same thing started to happen to him. But instead of offering to help them with the "monster," he agreed with them that it must be dangerous and by tiptoeing away from it with them he gained their confidence. He spent a long time with them in their houses until he could teach them, little by little, the basic facts which would enable them not only to lose their fear of melons, but even to cultivate them themselves.

To follow for a moment Nouwen's exegesis of this beautiful

story, Spirit speech adapts itself to the vernacular of the needy and stakes out a position of "solidarity" with them, is willing to suffer pain and uncomfortable "displacement" for their sake, and is committed to a "discipleship" that teaches at the same time as it learns.

In the midst of a canal named for love but twisted by greed into a channel of death, pastor Bruce Stearns lived out the Sufi parable, practicing its precept "to suffer with." When the people in Love Canal's second ring discovered that, if home is where the heart is, their hearts had been soaking in caldrons of poisonous chemicals, 80 percent eventually evacuated their dwellings for safer residences in other parts of Niagara Falls. But this pastor refused to budge from the parsonage, claiming that the only way he could faithfully minister to his congregation was to pitch his tent and cast his lot with theirs. "The way of safety is not always the path of service," he declared. His life spoke such a universal tongue of compassion that many bitter, hardened residents, dumped on with the sewage of our apathy, relearned the original meaning of the name "Love Canal." The gift of tongues, as Jesuit founder Ignatius Loyola testified in his diary, often comes in life at the same time as the gift of tears.

Compassion, or the voice of lives lived in common with others, is what made the evangelism, stewardship, and worship of the early church so uncommon (Acts 2:44–47). The early church was not concerned about making buildings full of people, but about making people so full of God's Spirit that they pooled their possessions, shared their meals, and happily listened to sermons. The first churches ministered within the context of community to the profoundest of human needs—the need to be fed, forgiven, hugged, and loved. Here in one another's homes Christians from the cities and the country gathered not merely for social togetherness but to build communities of the Spirit where are celebrated some of the most intimate things people can do together—break bread, pray, extend the kiss of peace, sing, and be silent.

Given this background, it comes as little surprise that

these early Christians were seen as subversive and dangerous, accused of "loving each other almost before they were
acquainted." What a beautiful indictment! The church
spoke, then as even now, the language of what compassion
can do—warmed by the glow it feels, comforted by the
assurance it knows, engaged by the commission it receives,
and living by the truth it espouses. When we find ourselves
in deep waters, when sorrows like sea billows roll, a Spirit-
filled church accepts us without reference to our past, our
social status, or our moral merit. Compassion is one of the
most subversive yet most sublime words in our religious
vocabulary.

5
THE GIFTS
OF THE SPIRIT

We walk in community, but we also walk alone. The 9 A.M. visitation of the divine Spirit in the upper room at Pentecost produced a rushing mighty wind that "filled all the house" and tongues of fire "resting on each one." As wind invaded the community, fire ignited each person. The definition of the Holy Spirit as the God who builds community does not diminish but indeed deepens the call for individual spirituality and personal piety. For although the Holy Spirit is relational, the gifts of the Spirit are individual. As gift, the Holy Spirit is given to create community. As giver, the Holy Spirit endows persons with spiritual gifts. The twelfth century is one of the most exciting periods of church history because it witnessed both the discovery of the self and the development of new forms of community. Jonathan Edwards is one of the most exciting theologians in church history because for him, in the words of Patricia Wilson-Kastner, "salvation was at once the most intensely personal and at the same time profoundly social experience one could have." Any religion that doesn't begin with the individual person never begins. But any religion that ends with the self is finished.

Two of the biggest questions raised by lay people trying to "walk in the Spirit" are: first, How does the Spirit lead? (or, How can I know the will of God for my life?); second, What are the tests of the Spirit that can distinguish the leading of the Holy Spirit from a host of human or unholy spirits? The Bible teaches us clearly that "whether you turn to the right or left, your ears will hear these words behind you, 'This is the way, follow it' " (Isa. 30:21). The capacity is there to hear the voice of the Good Shepherd and, what is more, to pick it out from the voice of the thief. We are enjoined to "test every spirit," for as I John 4:1 reads, "Do not believe every spirit, but test the spirits to see whether they are of God." A recent Gallup Poll revealed that 64 percent of the Protestants and 42 percent of the Catholics put the Holy Spirit either first or second when asked where they would turn to "test" their own religious beliefs. What does it mean to seek guidance of the Spirit? If you want to hear what the Holy Spirit is saying to the churches, where do you listen?

Lily Tomlin uses the joke in her act that if you talk to God you're sane, but if God answers you're crazy. The Holy Spirit enables us to hear God's answers, to put on the mind of Christ, or more boldly, to "think God's thoughts after Him" (C. F. D. Moule). The Spirit uses primarily four means to this end: circumstances, counsel, communication, and Scripture. All four are meant to be experienced in community, which is where the will of God is best discovered.

The Holy Spirit makes apparent the mind of Christ through circumstances. This conclusion has been a long time coming. I used to put almost everything down to happenstance, coincidence, being in the right place at the right time—and undoubtedly these things are part of it. But two scholars have helped me to see the hand of God more visibly in the events of our lives. Carl Jung is one of them. His concept of "synchronicity" suggests that what we call "coincidence" is often the coming together of events that really belong together. John B. Cobb, Jr., is the other. He contends that there is a "directivity" tugging at the heart of human experience that prompts the "synchronicity." There is a divine gravity pulling all living things toward a fresh future with new possibilities and grand surprises. Much of who we are depends on who we choose to become, and these choices take place within the context of circumstances that appear random, but are really the Spirit's "synchronicity" closing some doors and opening others.

The Spirit guides us in another way, through the community of faith, the tradition of the church, and the counsel of other believers. Discovering the mind of the Spirit is a social as well as a personal experience. Paul found this out on the Damascus road when he was literally blinded by the light of God's presence. He stumbled clumsily in the dark, powerless to discern his destiny, unable to fathom what had happened to him until the touch of another life brought sight and meaning and the Spirit to his life.

A third way the Spirit leads is through prayer or the breathing of the soul. Prayer ushered in the first Pentecost, and it ushers in the Spirit's presence in our lives as well as it oxygenates the soul. Communication with God does not yield absolute certainty, but it produces an "it feels right in the Lord" confidence that allows us to proceed with humble assurance.

A fourth way God speaks to us today is through the Scriptures. The Bible makes it very clear that the Spirit always leads us to do certain things. We waste a lot of effort in seeking Spirit direction about things the Bible already tells us God wants us to do. It is always the Spirit's voice telling us to forgive those who trespass against us. It is always the Spirit's intent that we upbuild the body of Christ and strengthen community. It is always the Spirit's prompting that we demonstrate God's love in our life, whether with our lips or our hands. Likewise, there is nothing mysterious about hearing the Spirit's voice when it comes to fighting injustice or oppression. In fact, our experience of the Spirit will be commensurate with the size of the problems we tackle. It is always the Spirit who arranges that Christians have, in Reinhold Niebuhr's words, a troubled conscience. Not because of unhealthy guilt complexes, but because Christians cannot be blissfully happy in a world of hatred and violence. Christians are those who wrestle with their consciences—and lose.

Circumstances, counsel, communication, Scripture—the Spirit speaks through their overlapping. But what if they don't overlap? They may come close, or even touch, but often it does not happen that all four overlap so that there is a clear picture of the Spirit's leading. Many will say, "Just live by the Book." But the Bible has little to say about the majority of the problems of contemporary life. What then?

Here is where "Spirit-led" language courts danger. Life is not a preprogrammed tape in some celestial computer, with our life assignment to develop the keypunch skills necessary to retrieve the predetermined decisions made for us by the Divine Programmer. God does have some very concrete purposes for us: that we grow in God's image, that we avoid mutilating the design. But in the majority of decisions we make in life, as John C. Haughey argues in his book *The Conspiracy of God* (1973), God seems more interested in the *context* of our choice than in the *content*. It matters more to God *that* we choose and *how* we choose than *what* we choose. In other words, as long as the context of our decision is informed, reconciling, compassionate, and impassioned, one decision is often as good as another. This is the meaning of Augustine's famous dictum, "Love God and do what you will." If the content of your decision is a love of God, then you can do what you want to do, because it will be a means toward the end of God's love. What may appear to be the Holy Spirit leading two Christians to different beliefs and actions may actually be the exercise of Christian liberty.

Or it may not be the Holy Spirit. One of the key issues throughout religious history has been, "What are the tests of the Spirit?" It is also one of the more prominent areas of division within the Christian community today—the relationship between the internal testimony of the Holy Spirit and external controls. "The Lord told me to" is a current refrain as the new Spirit consciouness has led more and more people to profess to speak God's mind. But it was a common claim in the past as well, and a solemn concern to those like the English author Samuel Johnson, who, speaking on the "inward witness" popular among eighteenth-century Methodists, growled that it was "a principle utterly incompatible with social or civil security. If a man pretends to a principle of actions of which I can know nothing, nay, not so much as that he has it, but only that he pretends to it; how can I tell what that person may be prompted to do? When a person professes to be governed by a written, ascertained law, I can know where to find him."

One of the most piercing memories of my high school years is of the closing service of a camp meeting where I was the organist. After a particularly sluggish sermon, the evangelist announced the invitational hymn "Softly and Tenderly, Jesus is Calling" and began wooing sinners to the altar. For the longest time (at least four verses) no one moved, but then out of the corner of my eye I thought I saw what looked like, but I knew couldn't be, my mother's best friend hitting the sawdust trail and proceeding toward the altar. She was the last person in the crowd I expected to go to the altar, because she was the first person I had always called on the phone to see if Christians still resided on planet earth. After I came home from school as a child, if I found no one there, I would panic, thinking that maybe Jesus had returned and I had been left behind. Her voice on the other end of the line calmed my fears, for I felt sure that Jesus would not leave her behind at the Rapture.

To my disbelief, it was she. And then, to my utter horror, she marched past the altar and ceremoniously plopped herself down by my organ bench, rocking on her knees in loud sobs and prayers, pleading with me to go to the altar. The Spirit had told her, she cried, that my past conversion was counterfeit and this was the appointed hour. The evangelist, seeing the prospect of his first and most conspicuous convert of the day, announced that we should all start over again and re-sing the six verses of "Softly and Tenderly." During that interminable period when I played the music for my own personal altar call, I contemplated for the first time the humiliation and cruelty of a bogus claim for the Spirit.

Every pastor has a favorite nightmare story about some person whom one never knows where to find, or about some faction in the church who think they have the Holy Spirit in their hip pocket. Every pastor also has almost daily conversations with someone who cries, "There are so many voices inside of me saying, 'The Spirit is leading here!' and 'No, the Spirit is leading there,' that I feel like screaming, 'Will the real Spirit please stand up?' " It's a good question. I John 4:1–3 teaches that every "inspiration" is not holy, and Paul himself twice refused to take the "Thus saith the Lord" advice of those professing to speak "through the Spirit" (Acts 21:4, 10ff.). We often say that the Holy Spirit dwells in our spirit, but how do we discern which is which? We need the ability to disentangle the Holy Spirit from *"Sieg heil"* spirits like selfishness, subjectivity, ambition, greed. For Christians have not been relieved of the responsibility of distinguishing the Holy Spirit from the "way that seemeth right," from misleading spirits.

Most traditions have developed mechanisms, although little known, for trying or testing the spirits. Roman Catholics, with their ordering of spiritual life by the church and their emphasis on the bishops as the guarantors of the Spirit, have had the least to worry about but some of the best guides to work with. Ignatius Loyola's "Rules for Discernment of the Spirits" is one such excellent aid to evaluating the promptings of the Spirit. The Quakers, who went farthest in the direction of subjectivizing the Spirit, fashioned a famous checklist of five ways the Spirit can be tested. Followers of Wesley, much tamer now than they once were in following the inward stirrings of the soul, have devised what they call a "quadrilateral of authority" (SERT—Scripture, experience, reason, tradition) that also works to brake the locomotion of careening spirits. Over against the Anabaptists and the Romanists and all others who taught that, in the words of Article 5 of the Augsburg Confession (1530), "we can attain to the Holy Spirit without the bodily word of the gospel and through our own preparation," the Reformers Luther and Calvin maintained the primacy of the Word.

The Reformed tradition waited until Jonathan Edwards, however, to develop clear public tests for inward experiences. Edwards' 1741 commencement address at Yale explicating I John 4:1 and entitled "The Distinguishing Marks of a Work of the Spirit of God" has still not been

surpassed for its depth of wisdom and breadth of useful-
ness. He propounds basically four tests for the theological
sifting of diamonds from dross.

The first test is: love for and confession of God the Father
and the Son. Where God is real, there is the Spirit. Wherever Christ comes alive, the Spirit is at work. The Holy Spirit
raises our God-consciousness and Jesus-consciousness, but
not our Spirit-consciousness. This is the primary christological test which asks whether a spirit points to Jesus as Lord
or to itself. The Holy Spirit does not glorify herself; instead
attention is deflected toward God and Jesus Christ. We are
most truly of the Spirit when we are least aware of the Holy
Spirit and most aware of Christ. This is why the Holy Spirit
has sometimes been called "God Incognito," or "The
Anonymous God." Michael Green has aptly remarked that
Christians "must remember not to do for the Spirit what He
does not do for himself and that is to seek the limelight."
The more we get to know someone, the more mysterious
that person becomes. As Emily Dickinson wrote of nature,
"those who know her, know her less / The nearer her they
get." Yet the closer many think they are getting to the
Spirit, the more arrogant and haughty they become about
their "Spirit-led" behavior. The Holy Spirit always has a
voice of humility.

The second test is: a love of truth as revealed in the Bible.
The Bible is the greatest protection the Holy Spirit has
given the church. Because of the constant exchange in the
church between Word and Spirit they refine and renew
each other. Almira Raymond, the wife of a missionary to
Oregon in the 1840s, wrote home to her sister about a
Presbyterian brother who felt called to herald Christ's
immediate arrival. When no one took his prophecy seriously, "he laid himself on the fire and literally roasted one side
believing God would heal it and convince us. But as soon as
he saw it was not healed he upbraided with the folly of
following false impressions and said the Word of God was
the only true guide. He was deeply pious, and doubtless
now rests in heaven." While Paul's aphorism that "the
letter kills, but the spirit makes alive" is widely quoted (II

Cor. 3:6), this poor missionary discovered that sometimes it is the "spirit" that kills and the "letter" that giveth life.

The third test is: a love of and commitment to each other. The social test of the Spirit is the great one for Edwards, and for Paul and Luke—is there a stitching back together of the seams that so easily rip in our relationships and fray the social fabric? What strengthens and unifies the community is of the Spirit; what destroys it cannot be. (Of course, there is some health and harmony that can only be born of pain and division). "Where the Spirit of the Lord is," Paul told the Corinthians, "there is freedom" (II Cor. 3:17). "For me there are no forbidden things" (I Cor. 10:23a, JB). We are either under liberty or under law, and those led by the Spirit have liberty. But then Paul goes on to state that there can be no liberty without restraint, no self-fulfillment without self-denial, for freedom is always a means to extending one's life for the community. "True, there are no forbidden things, but it is not everything that helps the building to grow" (I Cor. 10:23b, JB). In other words, our freedom is limited by our life together in community. "The love of Christ constraineth us" (II Cor. 5:14, KJV). Not everything upbuilds and uplifts the body of Christ. The Spirit can be finally confirmed and certified only in the company of others.

The fourth test is: a love of righteousness, a heightened sense of sin, and a turning from evil. Does the Spirit bear forth good fruit, promote agape, and reach out in service to neighbor and to world? The Holy Spirit may lead us all to different paths of righteousness: for one person prayer, for another the pavement; for one person the pen, for another the placard. But we are all pilgrims on the Samaritan road together.

There is another pressing question concerning the Holy Spirit and the person that follows from our discussion of the means and the test of the Spirit. What are the signs that someone's life has been kindled by the fires of the Spirit? The Bible presents two signposts of the Spirit: the gifts of the Spirit and the fruit of the Spirit.

"Now concerning spiritual gifts," Paul wrote in I Cor.

12:1 (KJV), "I would not have you ignorant." In other words, we had better get this right. *Charismata* is Paul's word. It is only found once in the Bible outside the letters of Paul, and it is used by Paul sixteen times. *Charismata* literally means gifts of *charis*, which in Greek points to God's unmerited love. *Charismata* thus are God's love gifts to us. One of the reasons I have held out so long in refusing to call my Pentecostal friends "charismatics" is that in Paul's sense of the word every Christian, not just a special party of believers, is charismatic. Every Christian has received love gifts of the Spirit, and every activity in the church, from the Bible study group "Soul Smithy" to the church softball team "Good News Bears," ought to be permeated with the spirit of these love gifts.

What are these love gifts, how are they apportioned, and which one(s) do you have? An inventory of the full range of spiritual gifts can be found in five passages (Rom. 12:6-8; I Cor. 12:8-10, 28; 14:6; Eph. 4:11). The most beautiful description of how the Holy Spirit apportions gifts in the human spirit can be found in Cyril of Jerusalem: "One and the same rain comes down upon all the earth, yet it becomes white in the lily, red in the rose, and purple in the violets and pansies, and different and various in all the several kinds."

As to one's own special gifts, imagine (as one radio preacher requested of his listeners) that it is time for Thanksgiving dinner. The whole family is gathered around the table, waiting eagerly for the arrival of the fatted bird. In from the kitchen comes a steaming platter filled with the turkey and all the fixings. Suddenly, the platter tips over and everything dumps onto the floor. Now watch how quickly all the spiritual gifts go to work. The prophet is usually the first one to speak. The Prophet: "Look what you've done! How are we going to eat? I've warned you before . . ." The Giver: "Don't worry about anything. I'll just go out and buy some more meat at the nearest open market." The Servant: "There's no need to get excited. I'll have this mess wiped up in a minute and no one will ever know anything happened." The Teacher: "The reason why the platter dropped is that two thirds of the turkey's weight was improperly positioned at the north end of the platter, causing the carrier to walk off-balance and trip on the rug." The Exhorter: "I see three things we can learn from this experience . . ." The Merciful: "Don't feel bad. I dropped many things myself over the years. Did I ever tell you how embarrassed I got . . .?" The Administrator: "O.K., now, let's get organized here. John, you go to the store. Mary, you find me some breadcrumbs . . ." The Sage: "God has a purpose in this disruption and disappointment." The Healer: "With a little cleaning up, this bird will be as good as new."

To deal with their family crisis, they needed all the gifts. In the words of theologian Hendrikus Berkhof: "*Charismata* are gifts to the individual, but they are never meant for private use." The gifts of the Spirit always put us in touch with others. They are all gifts of community, and the needs of the Christian community require all of them. The Holy Spirit is present to each person as a different gift—which makes us interdependent. We need each other if we are being truly filled with the Spirit. The anonymous author of a twelfth-century treatise writes: "Love in others what you yourself do not have, so that another shall love in you what he does not have, so that what either does shall be good for the other and those shall be joined in love who are separate in works." In church, our equality is our individuality. What makes us all equal in the body of Christ is what makes us all different. Thus our own special gifts are enhanced and at the same time humbled by the gifts of others. Without others, our gifts cannot be developed and deepened. With others, our gifts will be checked and limited. Someone has rightly said that God is wanting to do through you what he has not been able to do in all of the past and what he will not be able to do in all of the future. But how much God can do through you depends on whether your spiritual gifts are employed in the service of others, or self-employed.

Hence Paul's definition of "charismata" as a "service" (I Cor. 12:5). The Spirit's love gifts are not for personal enjoyment, employment, or edification. They are given for the service of others, the building up of the church, the communion of saints. When he spoke of his gift of scholarship, Martin Luther's words could have been those of Paul: "But if it is a gift of God, then it is entirely a debt one owes to love, that is, to the love of Christ. And if it is a debt owed to love, then I must serve others with it, not myself. Thus my learning is not my own; it belongs to the unlearned and is the debt I owe to them." A spiritual gift must not be divorced from the community of faith.

In fact, the very worst thing we can do is to cut ourselves off from the Spirit's sources and stockpile our gifts. This brings us to the so-called "Unpardonable Sin" of Matt. 12:31-32, the sin against the Holy Spirit. There are two kinds of Christians who read these verses: those who take them too seriously and those who do not take them seriously enough. Many of us have quaked under this teaching, the most blood-curdling thought in the Bible. In fact, Halford E. Luccock once listed "Things I Wish Jesus Had Never Said," and the "Unpardonable Sin" was one of them. It has messed up too many minds. Yet some need to take more seriously these words that thunder with doom—"Blasphemy against the Holy Ghost shall not be forgiven"—because they convey the shuddering truth that we can put ourselves beyond God's reach. There can be a crater at the center of the soul where God should be.

In a sense, of course, every sin is a sin against the Holy Spirit, for sin violates and frays the ties that bind us to God and to each other. Many, like the poet and hymn writer William Cowper, have been terrorized by the question: Was what I did or said heinous enough to make me guilty of having committed the sin against the Spirit? (The mere fact that Cowper raised the question ought to have dismissed it.) This question is sadly unnecessary, since we sin against the Spirit all the time and receive pardon equally afterward. The phrase "unpardonable sin" is also a tragic choice of words (besides being unscriptural), for the Bible nowhere says that any sin is unforgivable.

What these verses do say is that there is such a thing as an unforgiven condition which will always go unforgiven but is not unforgivable. The Spirit is a fragile life force that diminishes with each rejection—hence the repeated warnings not to "quench," "grieve," or "resist" the Spirit. We slough off the Spirit at our peril. We can succeed at elbowing the claims of others from our lives to the point where we can no longer hear or see or feel the Spirit. We can become so immersed in an egoistic world view that believing something outside of it is hopeless and faith is literally impossible. Just as a branch broken from a tree withers and dies, so a soul detached from the sources of the Spirit shrivels up and decays. If we forfeit the Spirit, we have nothing else to lose. Jesus' teaching about the sin against the Spirit was not intended to drag our minds to the mental hospital; rather it should function to beckon our bodies to church.

The gift of tongues is worthy of special attention. If there is one thing we have learned in the past decade or two, spirit-filled is not tongue-tied. Although a recent study by Cyril G. Williams claims that there is only one kind of tongues-speaking in the Bible, most scholars distinguish between two different kinds: that referred to in the book of Acts (chs. 2; 10; 11; 19), or xenoglossia (the speaking in a foreign language unknown to the speaker); and that referred to in I Corinthians (chs. 12–14), or glossolalia (the unintelligible vocalization of noncommunicative utterances). In all of history there have been no supported claims that anyone after the days of Acts (when unsought, uncontrolled, collective instances of xenoglossia occurred at the time of Gentile conversions) has ever received this gift. Modern tongues-speaking is glossolalia.

Contrary to popular stereotype, tongues-speaking is totally unrelated to one's mental health, emotional condition, social class, life situation, church affiliation, culture, civilization, or even morals (the people of the New Testament most noted for their glossolalia were also most noted for their carnality). Speaking in tongues has been reported in rituals of worship in ancient Egypt, Samaria, India, China, Ireland, Wales, and Africa, and in the universal ritual of lovemaking, when lovers speak to each other in nonsensical sounds. Some theologians are even convinced that when Paul speaks in Rom. 8:26 of the Spirit interceding for us when we do not know how to pray with sighs and groans too deep for words, he is referring to glossolalia. If they are right, it would doubtless be a surprise to many Christians to learn that they have been speaking in tongues all this time.

Although by the fourth century Chrysostom in the East and Augustine in the West deemed glossolalia dead and buried, scattered incidences of its practice survived throughout Christian history. For example, it occurred among the nineteenth-century Irvingites. A young skeptic of mixed motives attended their meeting one evening. Much to everyone's surprise, especially his own, he found himself speaking in tongues—and went forth in his new-found faith and became a Zoroastrian. Tongues may or may not be Christian; they may or may not even be religious. Both for Jesus, who never spoke in tongues but prophesied that people would, and for Paul, who himself spoke in tongues but prophesied that they would "pass away," tongues-speaking was nothing much to get excited about, and certainly nothing to brag about.

Paul's great standard of what are the higher and lower gifts is in I Corinthians 14 and Rom. 12:4-8. Simply put, does it edify the church? Waving this banner, Paul accuses the Corinthians of majoring in minors, of taking what is actually the gift of least importance, because it doesn't build up the body, and making it into the summit of Christian experience. Paul plays down the gift of tongues while boosting the gift of prophecy, or the ability to discern the Spirit's direction on a day-by-day basis.

But even then, Paul shows us a "more excellent way." Love is the sun around which revolve all the other gifts in the galaxy of the Spirit. Without love, spiritual gifts are wasted and worthless. "If the Pentecostal Church had spread love as they have spread speaking in tongues," Juan Carlos Ortiz has written, "the world would have written another history of this century." The hearts of "charismatics" may be in the right book of the Bible, but their heads are in the wrong chapter. Charismatic Christians (that includes all of us) need to stop living in the twelfth chapter of I Corinthians and step out into the thirteenth, where the most beautiful love poem ever written whispers to the soul the innermost secrets of the Spirit. In spite of its frequent appearance at weddings, this moving lyric does not chronicle the ways of two lovers. The love it describes is the love that the Spirit makes real in our life together as the body of Christ.

The presence of gifts that promote community may signify that the Spirit is present. ("Gifts" that do not are not the gifts of the Spirit.) But the absence of gifts does not signify that the Spirit is absent. The significance of a believer's "gifts" is judged by a believer's ninefold "fruit"—and it must be ninefold if the building of community is to grow. Love is the body of community. Joy is a community's laughter, peace its prayer, patience its hope, kindness its etiquette, goodness its mission, faithfulness its promise, meekness its spirit, and self-control its discipline. Nothing more need be said about a community that offers slim pickings of the fruit of the Spirit.

The fact that "fruit" is singular is important. There is only one fruit of the Spirit. That is love. All the rest are manifestations of love. The parallels between I Cor. 13:4-8 and Gal. 5:22-23 are more than accidental: "love is patient ["the fruit of the Spirit is patience"] and kind ["kindness"]; love is not jealous or boastful; it is not arrogant or rude ["gentleness"]. Love does not insist on its own way ["self-control"]; it is not irritable or resentful ["peace"]; it does not rejoice at wrong, but rejoices in the right ["joy"]; love bears all things, . . .endures all things ["goodness"]. Love never ends ["faithfulness"]."

6
THE ECSTASY
OF THE SPIRIT

Any discussion of the Holy Spirit in the life of the believer inevitably shades into a discussion of the "charismatic movement." A current joke says that there are three great lies in our time. First, "The check is in the mail." Second, "Of course I'll respect you in the morning." Third, "I'm from the government and I'm here to help you." Some would add a fourth, "I'm a charismatic and I'm a loyal member of First Church." Few issues are more fraught with fever than the place and propriety of the Pentecostal movement and its history of rapid spread in mainline Protestant and Roman Catholic churches.

At the beginning of this century, Pentecostals were as scarce as sunbathers in winter. In contrast, today looks like the summer of the Spirit, with Christians decked out in deep spiritual tans and sunburns. Nineteen percent of all adult Americans (over twenty-nine million people) consider themselves to be Pentecostal or "charismatic" Christians. One quarter of these are Roman Catholic, two thirds are Protestant. Viewed from any angle, these are astounding figures. Young people whose parents never could even get them to sing the hymns in church are now speaking in tongues. Protest marches have given way to Jesus rallies; teach-ins and sit-ins to healing services; peace signs and obscene gestures to "one-way" fingers; and before-work rounds of golf to prayer breakfast round tables. As this bloody, battered century is drawing to a close, the Pentecostal movement still stands as one of the most significant recent developments in twentieth-century religious life.

But who is a Pentecostal? Trying to define Pentecostalism is like picking up Jell-O with your fingers. The recent trend of fewer and fewer self-styled Pentecostals professing any history of speaking in tongues (only one sixth of all Pentecostal-charismatics claim the gift of tongues) makes the problem even more slippery, like picking up jelly. Some things we can quickly grasp. Pentecostals share with their Protestant and Roman Catholic counterparts the belief that the Holy Spirit makes the Scriptures come alive and motivates sinful people to come to Christ in humility and repentance. What has happened for us, by the power of the Holy Spirit, now happens in us. Pentecostals are also in agreement with mainline Christians that conversion (or justification) cannot occur without a personal reception of the Holy Spirit (Rom. 8:9; I Cor. 12:3b). Whoever receives and believes the gospel receives the Holy Spirit and is incorporated into the body of Christ.

Pentecostalism also shares with United Methodists, holiness groups, and some evangelicals the belief that there is a subsequent experience to conversion variously called sanctification, second blessing, second baptism, or second experience of grace, something which most Christians flatly deny although they do allow for subsequent "fillings" and for continued recallings of the believer to the charismatic fullness of the first act of grace. Pentecostalism differs from them—and this marks a Pentecostal—concerning what it is that evidences the experience they call "baptism in the Spirit." In short, all Pentecostals believe that Pentecost, unlike the Atonement, is repeatable.

It is helpful here to divide Pentecostals into hard and soft varieties: the hard Pentecostals believe that speaking in tongues is the initial, outward, normative sign of Spirit baptism and is distinct from and subsequent to conversion; the soft Pentecostals believe that whereas all Christians may have the Holy Spirit, the Holy Spirit does not have all Christians, thus the need for some kind of indwelling of the reality of living in the Holy Spirit in which tongues-speaking may occur but is not the normal experience to be expected of every Christian.

To avoid confusion we further need to distinguish at least two different segments of Pentecostalism, encompassing both hard and soft strands. First, the "classical Pentecostals" belong to those 150 or so organizations which emerged from the springtime of Pentecostal growth at Topeka, Kansas, and Azusa Street in Los Angeles at the turn of the twentieth century. They are organized, with their own denominational publications, theologies, and polities. Second, the "neo-Pentecostals" date from the charismatic sweep of the 1960s and have remained within their traditional churches where they participate in "charismatic renewal" activities in retreats and small groups. It is the upsurge of this second group in particular that has prompted Karl Rahner to observe that "divine fire is producing an awful lot of human smoke."

Why has it become so fashionable to look for the Spirit at this time in our history? Like its close parallel, the camp meeting phenomenon of the nineteenth century, neo-Pentecostalism can be interpreted as a metaphor for the changes and cultural transformations of contemporary American society. First, the neo-Pentecostal movement is an expression of a cultural shift inward where self-fulfillment is found through a range of religious options from Arica to Zen, offering rituals of self-absorption. While some observers like Daniel Yankelovich in *New Rules* (1981) see some evidence of a turning from self-esteem to social values, from a "Me" to a "We" society, most would find Americans still mired in what John R. Brokhoff has tagged "Burger King theology"—a "have it my way" faith that has wandered far from the hymn "Have Thine Own Way, Lord." The "revolution of rising entitlements" (Daniel Bell) has been a quest, focused on self, not for equal opportunity but for equal results. Grade inflation in school, the replacement of merit by length-of-service raises in business, and speaking in tongues in religion are all exhibitions of this insistent egalitarianism, loss of respect for exterior evaluation and control, and commerce in self.

Second, and somewhat related to the preceding observation, the neo-Pentecostal phenomenon can be understood as a critique on social sources of authority and an attack on our credentialism where, to be anything from a preacher to a plumber, one must obtain the proper credentials from the appropriate boards and be licensed by the approved experts. Pentecostalism promises direct access to the Holy Spirit, and speaking in tongues renders an immediate validation, available to everyone regardless of social status, education, or previous experience. The same sentiment which led a seventeenth-century scholar to complain, "It was never the intent of the Holy Ghost to make it a matter of wit and subtlety to know how to be saved," has led many Christians to despair of the intellectualism of the religious establishment. Just as in the 1970s people took their health into their own hands—jogging, popping vitamins instead of Valium, and reading Norman Cousins' *Anatomy of an Illness* (1979)—so lay people took religion away from the experts.

Third, neo-Pentecostalism represents a reaction against atrophied feelings at worship, against the substitution of cerebration for celebration, against bolted-down pews, sit-down services, stone-faced monologues, and sermon-proof congregations. Through the rediscovery of emotions, dance, praise, and the senses, the new figure of "the sensuous Christian" reflected the heightened spontaneity, instantaneity, and sensuousness of the time. The swing toward the expressive marks for some scholars also a rediscovery of the archetypically feminine side of God.

Fourth, neo-Pentecostalism represents a growing cultural disenchantment with words. The devaluation of our verbal currency is visible in the triumph of the sound-sight medium over the print medium, the fascination with body language, and the fate of two of the most misbehaved words in the past two decades—"honest" and "sincere." As Ella Fitzgerald finds in her "Memorex" commercial, there comes a time when words cannot express the sentiments of the soul, and just as some jazz singers lapse into "scat," some Christians lapse into their own "idealects" and speak in tongues.

Finally, neo-Pentecostals themselves, when asked about their amazing growth over the past two decades, claim it is a reaction to what is perceived to be an unprecedented moral and religious decline in America. The spouse of a minister in western New York was recently turned down for jury duty because her presumed "high moral standards" rendered her an unfit selection. It is incidents such as this, piled on top of each other, that have convinced many that America the New Jerusalem has become the old Babylon.

A sober assessment of the neo-Pentecostal phenomenon is only possible if we steer clear of the two ailments coined by Kenneth Cain Kinghorn, "charisphobia" and "charismania." Charisphobics are those people with such an irrational fear of charismatic activities that they have an eleventh commandment: "Thou shalt not commit a Pentecost." Moody Bible Institute in Chicago, for example, has posted in its men's and women's dormitories a set of "Emergency Instructions" for use in disasters like fire, tornado, air raid, bomb threat, suicide, and "charismatic activity."

Charismaniacs, on the other hand, are those people who so lust after religious experiences, seeking one spinal eruption of goosebumps after another, that they are guilty, according to the fourteenth-century mystic Meister Eckhart, of spiritual unchastity. High on the fumes of religious ecstasy, charismaniac evangelists are so drugged that they cannot be held accountable for what they say—"We're gonna fill you so full of the Holy Spirit that if a mosquito bites you, he's gonna fly away singing, 'There's Power in the Blood.'" Sometimes we need to keep reminding ourselves that it is the ill-digested piety of the charismaniacs, and not the Holy Spirit, that has the halitosis.

Because its contributions far outweigh its liabilities, we will mention the negatives of Pentecostalism first. An emphasis on the gifts of the Spirit and spiritual arrogance often keep company. Any Christian who has been looked down on as half Christian by unmannered, "full gospel" belligerents knows the feeling behind Zwingli's snide characterization of the Anabaptists: "They boast of the

Spirit." While Pentecostals enjoy their sense of being upper room disciples, the rest of us are made to feel left behind as manger shepherds. It is this charismatic condescension that has proven so disruptive in the local church and has led to church fights that make the War of the Pacific look like a Sunday school picnic. Irony is too gentle a word for the blistering fact that controversy over the God who builds community has been responsible for some of the bigger cracks in God's community.

Even within the "charmed circle" of charismatics themselves, the impression is sometimes given that here Christians are playing "Spirit, Spirit, who's got the Spirit?"—with everyone, trying to see in whose life the Spirit is most at work, and with no one's passion for spiritual gifts seemingly under divine control. We all need to be filled with the Spirit, but true filling only comes when we are empty, empty of pride, empty of jealousy, empty of prejudice, empty of greed. That's why one is tempted to say of being filled with the Spirit what used to be said of going to heaven: "Everybody talkin' 'bout heaven ain't goin' there."

One of my peeves with some neo-Pentecostals is that they forget they are members of the human race. Many of their "miracle" stories that abound seem bent on testing the limits of our credulity, their self-indulgence, and God's patience. There is both silliness and spookiness in the way the Spirit works, according to the testimony of many neo-Pentecostals, as if the Holy Spirit exists to defy for their benefit the laws of existence. There was something sadly tragic in the number of diseased and crippled brought backstage after the Beatles' concerts to receive their healing touch. There is something tragically sad about the requests for healing of cats, cars, and baldness phoned into prayer lines of the Church of Christ Electronic. Do we attribute it to amazing grace, or amazing arrogance, when someone professes never having to worry about a parking space, for God always makes one available? One begins to wonder whether it is the Rock of Ages or the Big Rock Candy Mountain where some neo-Pentecostals go for shelter in the time of storm.

One day I taught my two-year-old son, who enjoys joining me for morning bathroom chores, to be a "helper" and throw me the towel after my shower was ended. The only problem is that ever since that day I can expect to have a towel tossed into the tub anytime between the moment I turn on the water and the moment I step out of the shower. He has not yet learned the difference between the right moment and the wrong time to render assistance. The uncoordinated faith and pimply piety of some Pentecostals needs to be disciplined by good old-fashioned Reformed teaching on "The Uselessness of God." It needs to be understood that God is not a cosmic servant at our beck and call to make us more comfortable and happy; that when we use God we abuse God and thereby risk losing God (for the Spirit is as much quenched by intemperance as by rejection); and that our chief end in life is to "glorify God and enjoy him forever." There is a right time for intercessory prayer, but it is usually not when we're looking for a parking space.

Finally, the greatest weakness of neo-Pentecostalism is its theology, which—what there is of it—often hovers above the ground like an untethered hot-air balloon. For many neo-Pentecostal theologians, the whole of Christianity is Pentecost. The rest is commentary. Neo-Pentecostalism has not faced the anti-intellectual implications of a theology centered in emotion and experience. Among some neo-Pentecostals, moreover, "sickness" is virtually synonymous with sin—as if the Christian faith were a guarantee of immunity from suffering. The deeper you go into any theology that covers up the fragility of life and the finality of death, Auschwitz and Atlanta, with platitudes about the Spirit's loving protection "for me and my pals," the shallower it gets. At the first puff of real wind, such spirits disappear into the thin air of unreality. Most worryingly, the "as the Spirit moves me" school of faith can easily become an excuse for indifference and escape from social responsibility, a sort of hallucinogenic trip to heaven.

On the other hand, the positive aspects of the Pentecostal

witness have been enormous. Neo-Pentecostalism will represent for future historians a seismic force that shook the foundations of twentieth-century religous life. Before sending a watch to the repair shop, we are prone to shake it vigorously and give it one last try—often to have it return to functioning order. This is the way the Holy Spirit sometimes works with the church. And this is what the neo-Pentecostal movement has done to the mainline churches: shaken them up so that they can return to working order. As at the pool of Bethesda, the Spirit's stirring of the waters signals healing and growth. And not since the eighteenth-century Wesleyan revival has there been such a genuine stirring of the Spirit.

Neo-Pentecostalism has diagnosed the cataracts of formalism shading the spiritual eyesight of the mainline churches, and it offers a new vision into the wide world of the Spirit. For the same reason one conversion is not enough: we need a daily turning to God and dedication of our lives. So one Pentecost is not enough: we need fresh fillings of the Spirit for special challenges and everyday needs. At the chapel of the seminary where I teach, above the pulpit is a sounding board with a descending dove carved into it just above the place where the preacher stands. "Seeing with the eye of a dove," as Gregory of Nazianzus phrased it, invigorates and transforms not just the quality of our preaching but all of human life.

The neo-Pentecostal movement also exhibits a healthy spiritual claustrophobia that gets jumpy around small gods, cramped liturgies, and confining creeds. Convinced that there is more to the faith than what they have been around in the present, neo-Pentecostals have challenged Christians to say with Luther and Calvin, Wesley and Edwards, "We speak that we do know, and testify that we have seen." They have taken to heart Karl Barth's supply-side theology, according to which we can get too little of the pneumatic in the church, but never too much. The quest for superlatives, unfortunately diverted at times into a rogue pursuit of the spectacular, or a bogus belief that the surest indicator of apostolic succession is evangelistic success, has basically been a good thing as Christians have confronted new meanings of discipleship, surrender, spiritual stamina, wholeheartedness, and the ministry of spiritual gifts in the life of the church. Krister Stendahl calls the New Pentecostalism "high voltage" religion, contrasting it to the "small voltage of flashlight Christianity of traditional churches" that just isn't strong enough to make human spirits burst into flame. It is true that the heat from the incandescent Christians sometimes leaves the rest of us burned to a crisp. But better this than a refrigerated religion as stale as cold toast.

The desire to "live Pentecost" has also unleashed a new gust of ecumenical energy just when a fatigued ecumenical movement was crawling to a halt. The most ecumenical meetings in town throughout the 1970s were not those held in the sanctuaries of mainline churches, but the church-parlor prayer meetings, home growth groups, and weekend retreats of the Charismatic Renewal movement. Two of the most respected theologians of Pentecostalism have stressed that the sweep of the Spirit does not snatch Christians away from their churches, but makes them better church members. "Neo-Pentecostalism does not change any of our melodies," writes Swiss Reformed theologian Walter Hollenweger, "but it changes the rhythm and sometimes the key." Popular Belgian Cardinal Leo Joseph Suenens similarly contends that, to be most useful, the "charismatic movement" must dissolve into the bloodstream of the church.

The phenomenon of a twentieth-century Pentecost has also brought into question the long-standing assumption that the gifts of the Spirit ceased with the apostolic age. Such a view has always been too pat, too limiting, as if religious experience has gone downhill since Pentecost. Nineteenth-century theologian Horace Bushnell's contact with the tongues-speaking followers of Scottish Presbyterian Edward Irving convinced him that the Spirit must never be shackled. A similar conclusion marked perhaps the most thoughtful and surprising document to emerge from the mainline response to Pentecostalism, the 1970 Presbyterian report "The Work of the Holy Spirit." Spiritual gifts such as healing can take place through medical means—surgery, psychotherapy, hypnosis, or acupuncture. But sometimes God rolls away the stone.

Neo-Pentecostals have also awakened our minds to be open to unusual ways God may be speaking to us. Thomas Mann's charming distinction between "moon grammar" and "daylight grammar" can be expanded into a typology of how the Spirit communicates. The "daylight grammar" of the Spirit is quite familiar to us: the Scriptures, tradition, events, worship. But we have for too long closed the shutters on "moon grammar": small groups, prayer, silence, meditation, even dreams, called by Erich Fromm "God's forgotten language." Some have argued that the first special gift of the Spirit in the Bible was Joseph's ability to interpret dreams, although dream interpretation is really a gift available to everyone.

Neo-Pentecostals also know almost better than any other segment of the Christian community the meaning of joy, sweetness, excitement, and praise. Some of us back off from the Spirit because we can't stand the excitement. Similarly, some Christians won't eat sugar unless it is hidden in the middle of a very bitter pill. But there are some very sweet aspects to being a Christian (Jonathan Edwards' favorite word was "sweet"), and the Pentecostals who sing "Sweet, Sweet Spirit" speak from the soul. Jesus may have been a man of sorrows and acquainted with grief, but he was also a man of laughter and acquainted with joy. God is above all a God of enthusiasm, sweetness, joy, risk, openness. God's mortal enemies are complacency, sourness, mediocrity, discouragement, and boredom.

Anyone who has ever attended a Pentecostal worship service has been struck by the unaccustomed sight of worshipers glad they are there and having a good time. In fact, Henry P. Van Dusen was probably right when he said that Paul would have been more at home in a Pentecostal assembly than in a Protestant cathedral. In spite of the fact that Pentecostal worship, when it forgets that the Holy Spirit is already present, can degenerate into Baal worship with its conjuring up of the spirits, its sense of joy, excitement, explosiveness, and expectation of God's presence continues to infuse new vitality into the "body life" of churches.

7
THE SCOPE
OF THE SPIRIT

"How is the power of the Holy Spirit within the Christian community related to divine activity within the world as a whole?" Michael Ramsey poses one of the most serious problems in theology today: the scope of the Spirit. Does the wind blow only in the church, or do the breezes of the Spirit blow anywhere, fanning the world as well as the church? Can the Spirit's purpose of building community be reached through secular means, or is the range of the Spirit bounded by the religious community? Is the divine at work as much in the Bill of Rights as in the Beatitudes, in Hemingway as in Buechner, in the White House as in Riverside Church, in an antinuclear rally as in a Billy Graham crusade?

Theologians Norman Pittenger and C. F. D. Moule represent the best of two different opinions on the Spirit in their books, both entitled *The Holy Spirit* (1974 and 1978, respectively). Pittenger is a process theologian who believes that as "Life-giver" the Holy Spirit is a generalist, the source of all beauty, good, and truth in the cosmos. He tells the story of a child who asks, "Where does the sky begin?" and is told, "The sky begins in your lungs," in order to illustrate how the breath of the Holy Spirit spreads out from a human life to encompass all of existence. Pittenger resists any attempt to "canalize," "parochialize," or "churchify" the Spirit within the religious arenas of the person or the church. He joins theologians John Hick and John V. Taylor in contending that much of the Spirit's work in the cosmos, through atoms and molecules, genes and glands, "has nothing to do with religion in the narrower definition of that word." While the church may be the place of "disclosure in special clarity of what God the Spirit is *always* 'up to' in the world," Pittenger emphasizes the universality and cosmic range of the Spirit.

Moule's more biblically oriented treatment of this subject accents the specialization of the Spirit's activity in the church and the believer. The Old Testament speaks only twice (in Job and Psalms) about the Spirit as a cosmic or creative force, he contends, and the New Testament restricts the Spirit even further to the Christian community and the "new creation." Paul never mentions the Spirit in relation to the cosmos, and always joins the Spirit to Christ, never splitting the two but never blurring the difference. Biblical language only justifies speaking of the Holy Spirit's work as the bearer of redemption and "new life," although Moule confesses that "few would wish to deny that God's Spirit has been at work in all great creative art and utterance everywhere." Interestingly, Moule ultimately concedes that God's working in the church and God's working in the world are not mutually exclusive.

Pittenger and Moule articulate profound half-truths. Process theologians and liberation theologians, who reflect in their writings the most prevalent definition of the Spirit in contemporary theology—"God in action"—are correct in their Puritan insistence on the Holy Spirit's activity in the world. No one is devoid of the Holy Spirit; no one is without "common grace" (Luther and Calvin); "prevenient grace" (Wesley); "the Inner Light" (George Fox). God does not walk in the door only when we open it, for God's Spirit is already at work in every place and in every person as "the true light that enlightens every man" (John 1:9). "Where shall I go from your Spirit?" the psalmist sang; "or where shall I flee from your presence?" (Ps. 139:7). The ancient Hebrews encountered, time after time, a God who even worked through secular, political forces to bring them back to the fold. The pagan Persian King Cyrus is called "my shepherd," "his [the Lord's] anointed," an instrument of

God who conquered Babylon and sent the captive Hebrews back home (Isa. 44:28; 45:1). The Wisdom literature also reflects this sense of God as working in and through the natural and historical world. Second-century apologists extended the sphere of the Spirit into the enlightenment of the mind and the highest aspirations of the human spirit. And Calvinists have affirmed the Holy Spirit's restraint of evil and maintenance of a livable and beautiful world by working in the lives of the unregenerate.

But no matter how profound this half-truth, there is still the other half of the truth. Moule is right in saying that the Scriptures claim more content for the Spirit than just "God in action" or the source of imaginative and creative life. When the Holy Spirit is credited with all life's nobler impulses, the Holy Spirit colors everything and thus colors nothing. Moule is also on target when he homes in on the Spirit's unique ties to the activity of the "new creation." Moule echoes the circumspect judgment of George S. Hendry: "The New Testament knows no work of the Spirit except in respect to the historical manifestation of Jesus Christ."

The way out of this dilemma is the way back to an understanding of the Spirit as the God who builds community. The community of faith, the body of Christ, is where the Spirit can be seen and experienced most profoundly, but there are different levels of permanence, intensity, and clarity to the work of building community. And the Spirit of God is present wherever community is being fashioned, for the Spirit's work in church, persons, and world is united. Community is implicit in creation and is brought to life, made manifest, by the power of the Holy Spirit. The Holy Spirit thus roams the world, not randomly but intentionally, seeking to create communities of learning, reconciliation, compassion, and passion.

John Calvin was known to underline the work of the Holy Spirit in human creativity—in drama, painting, music, literature. In fact, some have seen in the Spirit's creative work of Genesis 1 the three canons of art: form, light, and beauty. One of the hottest issues in literature at the moment is whether art partakes in some degree of the divine, or whether art is free of morality and meaning. Flannery O'Connor defined art as "naming the things of God." Anthony Burgess, on the other hand, contends that art is art: "It means itself, no more."

One must be careful not to claim too much for the Spirit in the arts. Art is sometimes as liable to lead us to worship art as it is to lead us to worship God. For every Rembrandt whose paintings point us to God there is a Picasso whose paintings (especially his later ones) point us to Picasso. Art is also but a fleeting experience of the depths of the divine. As finely spun as a spider's web, the spell of art is as easily broken. By itself art is unable to do more than leave us "almost persuaded" with a lingering ache for forever in the pain of now. Yet it is also true that what is going on in the realm of art and music and fiction may be of more conse- quence to the building of community than what is taking place in the churches.

This is because all art is intrinsically social. There is an old axiom that says it takes two to make drama—an actor and an audience. The very process of creativity implies a social dimension, which is visible, for example, in the special community created between a poet and his or her readers. A lovely old story tells of a city that was to be built by music. One person tried to build it with a harp, another by a trumpet; and all of them failed until all played in symphony. The same reason why the anarchist Proudhon despised and attacked symphonic music (because of its "cooperative aspect") is the reason why all art is the devil's personal hell. For just as the melody of song affirms and amplifies the life of a single note, so all art is an offering to community, crossing the boundaries between solo and symphony, blending the contributions of the one into the greater life of the many. The creative work of the Spirit is the creation of community.

Is this not the effect of a Dostoevsky novel, Mozart quintet, Wright house, Donne sonnet, Ming vase—the building of bridges across languages, cultures, and nations, the drawing together into a family of humanity that is then ushered into the vestibules of truth? From the earliest evidences of the creative imagination at the Lascaux cave paintings to the modern graffiti that adorn a New York City subway, there is the autograph of the spiritual conscious- ness of the human psyche, its grasping for community, and the presence of the Spirit. All art is deeply spiritual. "One has to be so terribly religious to be an artist," griped D. H. Lawrence, who attributed his verse to a cooperative ven- ture between himself and "the wind that bloweth through me." Pianist Van Cliburn concurs: "Great art is nothing but prismed art of the eternal."

What makes music sacred is not the religious status of the artist, but whether the heart of the listener is in tune with the unbroken music of creation. The very music that could lead Albert Einstein to climb on stage, embrace Yehudi Menuhin, and shout to the audience, "Now I *know* there is a God in heaven" could lull Adolf Hitler to sleep. Beetho- ven's *Fifth Symphony,* which moved the French poet Claudel to exclaim after hearing it now he knew at the heart of the universe there is joy, left the pessimism of the French philosopher Sartre unchanged. The debate over Brahms's piety or Beethoven's pantheism fades into foolishness after one has heard the concluding section of Brahms's *German Requiem* or the thirty-eight notes of the trumpet call in Beethoven's lone opera *Fidelio,* both of which proclaim the resurrection more powerfully than a thousand Easter ser- mons. Although he was an atheist, the Romantic musician Berlioz composed the exquisite *Te Deum* and *The Child- hood of Christ.* Peter Shaffer's moving Broadway play *Amadeus* takes as its theme the Spirit's use of an ugly vessel of clay for God's glory. The Spirit can make even unbelief praise God, put us in touch with the mysteries of the universe, and seize people with the reality of community.

One of the most neglected areas in recent theology is the realm of nature and its relationship to God and persons. Is God in nature as Spirit? You decide. Two times in my ministry I have presided over interment services where the ashes were to be strewn outdoors. The first was for a fifty- five-year-old veterinarian, the picture of health and vitality, who died suddenly of a heart attack. A man of uncommon goodwill and friendliness, his presence was so captivating that the spirit and character of the church increasingly resembled his spirit and character. He had become to me a father, the kind of man I wanted to become, and with his death a part of my soul shriveled in despair. In shock we stood there in the meadow by his home, overlooking the lovely Genesee Valley, and silently watched as the wind took his ashes and scattered them over the land he loved. I trespassed on the silence with a mournful prayer that one would expect to hear from the lips of those who have no hope. But as we raised our eyes after my doleful "Amen," we were frozen in awe by the sight of two white butterflies which swooped down, hovered over the exact spots in the meadow where his ashes had fallen, and then flew away into the blue summer sky. A coincidence, or an epiphany, messengers of the Spirit to witness to a resurrection that selfish grief had forgotten?

A second occasion for the Spirit's presence in nature was the interment service for a beautiful twenty-two-year-old model who was tragically killed in a motorcycle accident. I had spent many hours struggling to help her escape the bondage of a free spirit that fluttered from flower to flower, sipping nectar from one budding experience after another, intoxicated by the honey of self-discovery. My closeness to her was strengthened even further during premarital counseling, when she and her fiancé decided to cancel the wedding, three days before the date. Her mother and I had just begun to rejoice in her newfound sense of purpose and resolve to return to college when the old yearning for one more fling with life, accelerator down, handlebars unguided, took over for the last time. Knotted up inside by the unfairness of it all, with silent murmurings and questionings about how this could happen just when she was getting her life back together and her emotions under control, I stood in a wildflower garden on her parents' farm and stretched out my hand to strew her ashes. Suddenly a mourning dove, its tranquil observance of our ritual disturbed by the movement of my hand, flew out of the red pine tree above my head, circled around the garden, and then gracefully glided off into the woods. A happy happenstance, or an epiphany, a message from the Spirit that the peace of God, which surpasses all human understanding, should bind our minds and hearts together? "When the soul listens," priest-poet Guido Gazell writes, "everything that lives has a tongue and speaks."

The tracks of the Spirit can even be traced to the material things that support human community. St. Simeon ends with a surprise note when he prescribes a course of action for those who want to "pray with a serene and pure heart": "Make your peace with God, with your own conscience, with your neighbor, and with every object you handle." The popular B. J. Thomas gospel song "Using Things and Loving People" gives illegitimate birth to simple and ultimately sacrilegious notions about a Christian's relationship to created things. In the traditional trinity of evils, the world, the flesh, and the devil, two out of three God blesses ("God so loved the world," "the Word became flesh"), leaving the devil to his own devices. A crying infant in an innkeeper's stable cast a halo over all of creation, making the Bible a materialistic book and Christianity a materialistic religion.

Paul's widely quoted distinction between "flesh" and "spirit" is misinterpreted as a contrasting of the material and the immaterial, as if matter were spirit's opposite and one canceled out the other. Rather, for Paul it is a dichotomy between the mortal ways of self-centeredness and the eternal ways of living in the family of God. Any pastor who has ever counseled a pregnant wife about whether or not to turn off the respirator on her twenty-seven-year-old husband, who has a cerebral hemorrhage and no EEG reading, can testify that matter is an important part of spirit, and love for the body is a big part of life. Matter and spirit God has joined together; anathema to any who put them asunder.

What is so incredible about this God of ours is that God says we need not feel guilty about our love and grief for what *The Sound of Music* called "favorite things." The Protestant hang-up about acquisitions, artifacts, and body movements cuts against the basic spiritual need for physical objects and a gestural language of greeting, adoration, humility, and worship. An Episcopal colleague tells the story of kidding his Altar Guild before an upcoming wedding, telling them that they missed a spot on a brass cross, only to have these highly intelligent and sophisticated people take him seriously and scour the sanctuary with their ministrations. There is a basic human need to do something physical on behalf of the spiritual, whether such gestures be shining brass crosses or dressing up for church. Materiality is integral to spirituality.

"Love objects" occupy an important part of community. Every family has them, and if lost or stolen, they are mourned and missed. An heirloom, a letter, a chair, a bottle of wine, these objects can cease to be "signs," in poet Paul Valéry's fine phrase, and become "significances." Psychologists call this "cathecting," the process by which things become a part of us, enhancing our growth, comfort, and enjoyment of life. The relationship that develops between us and things is called a "cathexis." Or one can use a more romantic word, the Arabic *baraka*, which conveys even better the "blessedness" and friendship that develop with places and things after years of tender loving care.

This is not the place to debate Alfred North Whitehead's assertion that matter is at bottom spiritual. The modest claim here has been that there is a spiritual dimension to matter, that "things" can be made to minister to human need. It is the Spirit of God who implants a tongue in the things of this world and blesses community through a smoking mountain, a burning bush, a loaf of bread, a chalice of wine, a font of water, even (Luther would insist we add) good German beer and sausage. The Spirit comes to us and brings us together through material consolations. For community is not limited to human members. We live in community with trees and books, sand and silicon chips, cats and tennis racquets, all of which can make us feel more at home with our universe and with each other. It is not just people and the natural order that share a common life and future, for feminist theologians have taught us that we are

partners with God in creation. Both natural and manufac-
tured things share the same boat with humans. Whether we
sink together or sail together depends in no small degree on
whether the relationship we strike up with "things" is
based on mutuality or superiority, honor or greed. It is
consumerism, not Christianity, that gives the word "materialistic" a bad name.

The Spirit of God is also at work through the historical
process to keep the gospel alive and to keep the church in
line with fuller disclosures of the truth. There is no place in
the Christian tradition for "as it was in the beginning, is
now, and ever shall be" theology. God's Spirit has not been
embalmed in a book, nor has God's voice been entombed in
a century. It is not just holy ones of old who spoke as they
were moved by the Holy Ghost. Holy people of today
continue to speak as they are inspired by God's Spirit. In
John Robinson's words of farewell to the Pilgrims, "I am
verily persuaded the Lord hath more truth and light yet to
break forth *out of his holy word.*"

To have this hope, this great expectation, does not mean
that we go so far as the Shakers, who were reluctant to
commit their beliefs to writing because they believed
God's revelation was progressive. The Spirit's work in
history is not a matter of new revelations but of fresh
interpretations of old revelations that were there all the
time but were glazed with the delusive assumptions of the
past. Jesus said the Holy Spirit will bring to the remem-
brance of every age "all that I have said to you" (John
14:26). The Spirit uses history as a cloth to continually
polish our perceptions so that the truth of living, if not
always our living of truth, becomes more brilliant and more
illumined. For example, the concerns that dominate the
Old Testament do not bear the same importance when we
get to the New Testament. Likewise, as the church historian Jaroslav Pelikan writes: "No one may take the position
on slavery the New Testament does and call it Christian." A
similar case could be made for Paul's position on women.
Because of the Spirit's work through the historical process
to refine and reform the community of faith, we must always

be open to growth in the knowledge of truth without succumbing to worship of the golden calf of novelty. "I have yet many things to say to you," Jesus told his disciples, "but you cannot bear them now. When the Spirit of truth comes, he will guide you into all the truth" (John 16:12–13). Truth is approach, not arrival.

Ever since Peter's sermon at Pentecost, Christians have faced the challenge of other faiths. But never before has the question of the Spirit's presence in other religions been such a carpenter of conundrums. Does the Spirit reveal God only through the Christian religion, or do religions such as Buddhism, Hinduism, and Islam also evidence the disclosure of the Spirit? As Kierkegaard and Nietzsche have revealed, whatever answer we give this terribly uncomfortable question will have a forceful kick to it. The jolting punch comes from the political as well as the theological implications of either a parochial or a cosmopolitan Spirit.

The Christian tradition can be very glib in its "the truth, the whole truth, and nothing but the truth" mentality, although often there has been a search for loopholes. Calvin, for example, gave a yes-no-yes handling to this hot potato: yes, the Spirit is operating in other religions to preserve order and dignity in the world; no, this is not enough for salvation; yes, there may be a "secret elect," so one can never be sure about the ultimate destination of a person of another religion. But for the most part the tale of Christian encounters with other religions makes rather grim going. Far from benign have been the effects of casting other religions into the pits of darkness and the depths of hell—social intolerance, cultural imperialism, theological triumphalism, religious persecution, racial bigotry.

The refusal to see the dispersal of the Holy Spirit in other religions has been made increasingly difficult today by a pervasive religious pluralism that is here to stay. We rub shoulders every day with people from different faiths, necessitating what sociologist Peter Berger has called *The Heretical Imperative* (1979). It is not the challenge of modernity but the "contestation" with a panorama of religious possibilities that has the most to teach today's faith,

Berger writes. It is a lesson we shall learn one way or another. There are more Muslims than Methodists in Britain right now, and tomorrow Christianity will boast a smaller slice of the religious pie than ever before. Challenged to "think globally and act locally," we find ourselves more and more swept into conversations with religious people who once we would have had to travel halfway around the world to find, but who today live next door.

The Christian response to religious pluralism has not been uniform. One reaction has been to bolt the doors of faith and keep yelling "pagans" into the ears of non-Christians, excluding from God's smile 99,999 out of the 100,000 or so religions produced by humans since their beginning. The problem with this position is that, first of all, Jesus scolded those who strutted it (Matt. 7:20; 15:8). Second, it fails to consider the fact that by its own definition the person Christianity names itself after was a "pagan." In Julius Wellhausen's famous words, "Jesus was not a Christian but a Jew." Third, the three billion non-Christians in the world right now are less objects for mission than subjects of God's love. The love that caused Jesus to die for these people is a love that never runs out, never even runs low, but is always running over. Unless we want to argue that God's love freezes in certain climates or that we can outlove the Lord, we had better be careful how we treat them, talk about them, and haughtily dismiss their religions as "merely" a delusion.

The other extreme has been to sink into a courteous relativism where "all roads lead to God" because it is believed that all religions are equal and should be brought together (a kind of theological UN based on "one nation, one vote"), or that all religions share a common denominator (an old-fashioned Enlightenment idea that still circulates with Wilfred Cantwell Smith), or that every religion can boast only partial awareness of the truth (philosopher of religion John Hick), or that more than one religion can be true even if contradictory (this position was made famous by the philosopher Karl Jaspers). The problem with these

positions is that they contradict the magnificent achieve-
ment of monotheism in the Old Testament (Deut. 6:4) and
the New Testament teaching about Jesus as "the way, the
truth, and the life." They also effectively dissolve all
substance from the meaning of the word "truth."

The most popular way out of this dilemma has been to say
that the Spirit works in all religious traditions to produce
what might be called honorary disciples or a salvation by
mistake. The early Christian philosopher Justin Martyr was
the first to play with such notions when he paid tribute to
the thinking of certain pagans by calling them "Logos
Christians." Tertullian, impressed with the loving disposi-
tions of certain people, coined the concept of the "instinc-
tively Christian temperament." More recently, theologians
have talked of an "implicit faith," the "latent church," and,
most widely quoted of all, the Roman Catholic theologian
Karl Rahner's concept of "anonymous Christians." "Anonymous Christians" are non-Christians in whom the Spirit is
at work incognito so that they act like Christians even
though they have no conscious commitment to Christ. To
embrace someone as an "anonymous Christian," however,
is to give them the kiss of death. It overrides their own
commitments, condescendingly judges them by ulterior
standards, dismisses the integrity of their faith, and denies
them the respect of calling them the name they have
chosen. One does not have to be a Christian if one does not
want to be.

In this high tide of pluralism it is high time for Christians
to uncover ways of affirming the particularity of their faith
while recognizing the universality of God's Spirit. The
New Testament claims that God is not without a witness
anywhere, that God has spoken "in many and various
ways," or in the words of the prophet Joel, the Spirit is
poured out upon all flesh. The Light has been shining so
that no one is beyond the reach of the Holy Spirit. The lives
of non-Christians like Lao-tsu, Gandhi, Black Elk, Malcolm
X, Simone Weil, and Dag Hammarskjöld bear compelling
testimony that it is not only professing Christians who
experience God and reflect the power and presence of

God's Spirit. Leslie D. Weatherhead's daring question is worth pondering: Who is closer to this God of ours we call "love"—the cold, callous Christian who passes by need and lives selfishly, or the warm, compassionate non-Christian who stops to help and lives generously?

At the same time that we honor in other religions the Spirit's movement, which knits its members into communities of love and faith and hope, we must not abandon our belief that Jesus is the Savior of the world and the Lord of all life. Indeed, I would argue that only those who stand tall with a vital sense of their own heritage and a strong religious identity are able to appreciate or learn from the spiritual experiences of others. Paul Tillich conceived the great principle of "We particularize in order to universalize." Just as the particular Christ of Palestinian Judaism made way for the universal Spirit, so true hospitality to God's presence in other faiths is conditioned by our particularism about our own.

A rabbi in Rochester, New York, responded to a reporter's question about the Jewish community's reaction to the vigorous evangelistic thrust of Key 73 (in 1973) by stating his conviction that strong Christians make better neighbors than weak ones. They may be out to convert you, he said, but you know where they are, they take your faith seriously, and they relate to you from a position of strength. There is nothing to be embarrassed about in believing the incarnation to be the normative revelation of God or that the Spirit labors more decisively in Christianity than in other religions. Indeed, if I felt that any religion were closer to the truth and did not go over to it, I would be a hypocrite in reverse. The worst neighbors one can have are truth's tramps, wandering from religious fad to religious fancy, hobos of the divine spirit who pitch their tents with whoever will feed them. The unparticularized love for everyone and every place is a love unrelated to earth.

The Christian does not live a stateless, churchless, or orphaned existence. We live in a definite country, come from a particular family, and follow the true Savior. If there is one thing we have learned from ethnic theologies, it is that beliefs are and should be shaped by the social context. But the Christian also has a commission that prevents withdrawal into the isolated hinterlands of the homeland. Instead, Christians will live, in Donald MacKinnon's suggestive words, on the "borderlands," where they can cross frequently into other countries, tour the truths of their habitats, celebrate the "converging spirits" that they discover, and shamelessly proclaim the unsurpassed beauty of the places where they live.

My favorite way of visualizing all this is inspired by a comment penned by the Romanian novelist Petru Dumitriu: "Yes, God is also dry land, dear fish, but if you try to climb out on dry land you will soon learn that . . ." The giant snag in Dumitriu's alluring analogy is that it destroys the concept of mission—that is, unless we classify the type of fish as *Anabas*. *Anabas* is a genus of fish that periodically leaves the water and climbs trees. The Holy Spirit so constitutes disciples of Christ that we become "anabas" Christians. There is only one atmosphere in which I can live—without Christ I die. But I am also called, like the climbing perch, to make myself vulnerable to other religions, to enter into friendships with the birds of the air and the animals of the land, to acknowledge that God hears their prayers, to recognize that my religion as well as theirs stands under the judgment and mercy of God, to join with them in fighting the quasi religions that threaten every faith, to have my own spirituality enriched by exposure to the profound truths in their faith, and, last but not least, to bring to their light the unshown Christ.

The forays of friendship by anabas Christians into other religious traditions do not require that we be open to "conversion" if true understanding is to occur. This requirement is the position of many theologians today, and in particular those who have employed the technical term "epoche," which refers to the joint suspension of beliefs during dialogue. Anabas Christians may find their own experiences of God illumined and enhanced by the insights on meditation gleaned from the sky and the land, but they also know that Jesus is not one option among many Saviors of the sky and Lords of the land. Anabas Christians also are very aware that if they do not return to the water where schools of other believers can sustain and nourish them, they will die.

Nor do anabas Christians try to drag the birds and the animals back into the water with them, except perhaps for a swim. The land and the sky have their own colors and customs, foods and songs. Those who have responded to our testimonies from the treetops will be led by the Spirit to return to their own natural habitats. What kind of bodies of Christ will spring up there is between them and God.

Perhaps the major preoccupation of theologians in the 1960s and 1970s has been the examination of human history and cosmic life as the arenas where the Holy Spirit is transforming existence into the likeness of Christ. Many theologians who argue about much else agree that the Holy Spirit is the Spirit of the future, pulling this world, often kicking and screaming, into the world to come. To give up on the future, or not to work for the future, is not to live in the Spirit. In fact, this is why only the third member of the Trinity is called "holy," for the essence of holiness is social and ethical—truth and beauty in action.

"The business of the Spirit," Paul R. Fries writes, "is to annex all of existence for the Kingdom." Jesus' kingdom is the power of the Spirit to help this world walk away from yesterday in a new path, with a new peace, among a new community, and toward a new future. The Spirit moves outside the church to bring to pass Jesus' prayer "Thy kingdom come," and to indict economic, political, and social systems that destroy community. The doctrine of the Holy Spirit is the generator for biblical ethics.

The major frustration in life is that we shall never get enough of the Spirit to satisfy either God or ourselves. There are certain Hebrew and Greek words that every Christian should know (e.g., *shalom, hesed, metanoia, koinonia, kenosis*), and Paul's word *arrabon* is one of them. The Holy Spirit is the "pledge," "security deposit," "first installment," "down payment," of God's coming kingdom (II Cor. 1:22; 5:5; Eph. 1:14). Christians who live the life of the Spirit enjoy the "firstfruits" of the future harvest (Rom. 8:23). They have received God's *arrabon*, which guarantees the final inheritance. But the *arrabon* is not a complete payment. Christians do not receive it all, which is why those who boast of the "fullness" of the Spirit speak utopian foolishness. Anyone who has ever tried to help others live in the power of the future resonates with a social worker's sigh about the power of sin, as quoted by Helen Oppenheimer: "We were put into the world to do good to others, but what were the others put here for?" The "fullness" of the Spirit is for the future; to be full of the Spirit is for the present.

We used to talk of "Christianizing" the social order. Today we talk of "liberating" a contrary culture. But whatever vocabulary we use, Christians are called to be the Spirit's confederates in countering such cosmic adversaries to the consummation of an eternal Pentecost as oppression, injustice, poverty, and prejudice. In spite of the fact that many liberals are still fighting the battle, liberalism actually won the war in the '60s and '70s—social action stands at the center, not the periphery, of the Christian faith's agenda. Christianity is a religion of both inner impressions and outer expressions. Christians may not all be ordained clergy, but they are all foreordained ministers with a social apostolate to sanctify or make holy all of life—social structures, persons, nature, things—so that life either channels God's love or makes way for God's judgment. The same Spirit who drove Jesus (literally, "threw him out") into a war with the devil in the wilderness drives us into waging what Percy Dearmer has called "a spiritual equivalent of war" against all that destroys community today and delays the establishment of what economist Hazel Henderson calls a "SHE" society tomorrow—"Sustainable, Humane, Equal." Jerry Butler, the Buffalo Bills' all-star receiver, posed a question at a Lenten breakfast at our church that resounds with urgency for all who share in the Spirit's struggle: "Are we making it easier for us to live, or harder for our children to survive?" Whether our children will grow up or blow up depends on how we answer that question.

Two dangers quickly threaten. One is that, instead of the gospel turning the world upside down, the world turns the gospel upside down. Christians are called never to be of the world, but always to be in it; never to merely cheerlead culture, but always to try and transform it. When we forget Jesus' question, "What do you more than others?" we reduce the Holy Spirit to our social conscience and religious consciousness, and religion becomes a social service of human-helping and problem-solving. Our world needs more than a drop-in center here and a drug clinic there. The human spirit is not simply a fragment of the Holy Spirit. The Golden Rule cannot be a substitute for the Apostles' Creed.

Yet those who counsel "Just put it in God's hands" forget that we are God's hands. The Puritan doctrine of "means," which says that God has no hands but our hands, is not a do-it-yourself social ethic. The Spirit miraculously multiplies our baskets as we divide with others what small resources of bread and fish are ours. The Spirit's confederates are people who are willing to divide that God may multiply, to descend into hell to raise earth to heaven—but God's Spirit leads and sustains them; otherwise they could not stand the heat. Christians ought never to forget the paradox that the coming kingdom is both a blessing from God and a bounden duty of humanity, a divine gift and a human task.

The second danger is related to the first. There is visible in some quarters a spiritual tic that twitches in ecstasy every time it is stimulated by the sight of some liberation movement improving human life. The surprising element in Jesus' account of what will happen at the Last Judgment, a biblical passage of unsurpassed artistry and candor (Matt. 25:31-46), is that some people will find themselves on God's side who didn't expect to be there. The temptation is to jump the gavel on heaven's Supreme Court and welcome into the Spirit's chambers all who visit the prisoner, clothe the naked, feed the hungry, and advance liberation. Some

Southern theologians were convinced that the Confederacy was the bearer of the Spirit in history. Some German Christians saw in Hitler's rise to power the handwriting of the Spirit. Some scientists were so excited about the potential for good of America's first nuclear test that they baptized the explosion "Trinity." And one Christian missionary organization so reflexively kneeled before every sign of liberation that it would later regret having hailed Idi Amin's efforts at "reform" and "reconciling" as a "true miracle of the Holy Spirit."

In direct contrast there is the more familiar story of those who refuse to see God's Spirit working unless among PEWS (Protestant, Evangelical, White Suburbanites) or until all socialistic or Marxist or noncapitalist snags have been combed out. How many times in history has the Spirit been grieved and quenched by the refusal of Christians to support radical change? The Spirit takes risks in dealing with this world, conscripting allies wherever they may be found. This means that the work of the Spirit is never straight, predictable, or safe.

The Spirit who struggles with the powers of evil challenges us to join in the struggle to create communities of meaning, communities of covenant, communities of Spirit. There are many who would tie a white flag around the future, voices of death that say nothing can be done until Jesus returns, things have progressed too far to ever make a difference, the best you can do is take care of yourself, you've done your best—now it is someone else's turn. But in the words of the ancient proverb, "The leaves may want to rest, but the winds keep blowing."

QUESTIONS
FOR DISCUSSION

1. THE POWER OF THE SPIRIT

1. What did Jesus mean when he said that it was good for us that he go away? Interpret Bishop Charles Gore's comment: "The Holy Spirit comes not so much to supply the absence of Christ as to accomplish his presence."

2. Think of all the different kinds of power that operate in the church. Which ones constitute "relational power," and which ones "unilateral power"?

3. In what ways should Christians be different from non-Christians? What are some of the forces of conformism at work in contemporary Western societies? How high are the costs of resistance?

4. Eduard Schweizer calls the Holy Spirit the "God Beyond Our Control." How do we try to control God, and in what ways does God confound our efforts? Give some personal examples of sudden surprises the Spirit springs on you.

5. Why do we need the device of talking about the Holy Spirit? Why not just talk about God, or God and Jesus Christ?

2. THE DIVINITY OF THE SPIRIT

1. In what ways do you think the *filioque* debate has been a constructive or a wasteful expenditure of Christian energy?

2. How does the conception of the Trinity as God in community alter how we understand, experience, and serve God?

3. Why is it said that only a suffering God can help? How would someone who is dying of lung cancer pray to a God who has never suffered?

4. What is your reaction to the statement that the Holy Spirit should never be referred to as "it"?

5. Christians have been charged, despite their public confessions of faith, with being practicing unitarians. To what extent is it accurate to say that when it comes to the Trinity, we contend for the doctrine but deny the experience?

6. Discuss John Leith's thesis that the following three prevalent kinds of unitarianism distort how we relate to God and to each other: "Unitarianism of the Father, of the Creator, leaves out of account the Redeemer and Sanctifier. The unitarianism of the Son forgets the Creator and Sanctifier. Finally, the unitarianism of the Spirit becomes absorbed in the work of God in the inner life of the believer to the exclusion of his other works."

7. What difference will it make in the Christian life if we add the concept of the Motherhood of God to that of the Fatherhood of God?

3. THE HOME OF THE SPIRIT

1. Discuss the claim that it is possible to enjoy a private religion and to be a solitary Christian. Can a person be a Christian and not be a member of a community? Why, or why not?

2. How would it change our patterns of living (e.g., worship, ethics, devotions, etc.) if we really lived the belief that "the Holy Spirit is God between us"?

3. What do you think about the proposition that religious experience is uncommon today, even in church? Define "religious experience."

4. What is the difference between the mysticism of the divine and the mysticism of the human? Describe your last

mystical experience.

5. Romans, chapter 8, the handrail of the New Testament, contains some of the most powerful words in all of the Bible (verse 16, for example). What makes them so powerful?

6. What does it mean to live in the Spirit without knowing it? In what ways could this ever have happened to you?

4. THE LANGUAGE OF THE SPIRIT

1. What does it mean to call someone spiritual? What should it mean?

2. Draw up some rules for fighting fair in church.

3. If any church in any community resolved to live completely in the Spirit of God for one week, how would that community be different?

4. Who are today's lepers?

5. Why do we speak of Jesus as "our Savior" and God as "our Father" but never of the Spirit as "our Spirit"?

6. Discuss the hypothesis that people have basic needs that must be met, and that if these are not fulfilled in church they will be met elsewhere. To what extent do sports events, rock concerts, movies, cults, etc., address these fundamental needs of human existence?

5. THE GIFTS OF THE SPIRIT

1. Look around you and identify the gift of the Spirit you see embodied in each person. Do the same for the ninefold fruit of the Spirit. Let each person declare the fruit they most want God to produce in them.

2. How are personal freedoms limited by our life together in community?

3. Would the Spirit ever lead a Christian to break any of the Ten Commandments?

4. Are Christians most truly "charismatic" when they are most aware of the Holy Spirit, or when they are most conscious of Christ? In what ways?

5. The Bible gives at least five major commandments

about life in the Spirit. Discuss them: (1) Walk by the Spirit (Gal. 5:16, 25). (2) Pray in the Spirit (Jude 20). (3) Grieve not the Spirit (Eph. 4:30). (4) Quench not the Spirit (I Thess. 5:19). (5) Be filled with the Spirit (Eph. 5:18).

6. What protection does the Holy Spirit give the church against counterfeit spirits?

7. Discuss this thesis: "The Holy Spirit leads believers to different conclusions about the same issue."

6. THE ECSTASY OF THE SPIRIT

1. What will be some of the far-reaching effects of this "Age of the Spirit" in the life of the church?

2. In what ways does the Pentecost Spirit thrive when the church lives as a majority voice in culture? As a minority voice?

3. Why are there so many biblical associations of the Holy Spirit with intoxication?

4. Locate the universal appeals in neo-Pentecostalism that cut across all economic, social, and religious barriers.

5. The eighteenth-century theologian John Fletcher found himself crying out one day, "O Lord, either enlarge the vessel or withdraw thy Spirit." What would it be like to know such a person, and how would that person be different from the majority of Christians?

7. THE SCOPE OF THE SPIRIT

1. Discuss this proposition: "God is biased on behalf of the poor and oppressed, and against the affluent and secure."

2. Evaluate the claim that every effort to combat oppression, injustice, and poverty is the work of the Spirit.

3. How would you defend the "Christianization of society" as a valid goal for Christians? In what ways can the widely publicized "secularization" process spell not an end of Christianization, as Hendrikus Berkhof argues, but a continuation of the process by different means?

4. How would you argue for or against the belief that it is

God's will that all the peoples of the world be of one religion?

5. How do you respond to Peter Berger's statement that "one seriously engages another religion if one is open, at least hypothetically, to the proposition that the other religion is true . . . [if one is open] to change one's own view of reality"?

6. If someone today took the position the Bible does on slavery, would that person be called a Christian? What does the Bible say? And what is the "Christian" position?

BIBLIOGRAPHY

1. THE POWER OF THE SPIRIT

Barth, Karl. *The Holy Ghost and the Christian Life.* London: Frederick Muller, 1938.

Brown, Dale W. *Flamed by the Spirit: Biblical Definitions of the Holy Spirit.* Brethren Press, 1978.

Coffin, William Sloane, Jr. "Fire or Fire." *Sermons from Riverside,* May 14, 1978.

Duncan, George B. *The Person and Work of the Holy Spirit in the Life of the Believer.* John Knox Press, 1975.

Loomer, Bernard. "Two Conceptions of Power." *Process Studies,* Vol. 6 (Spring 1976), pp. 5–32.

Meyer, Paul W. "The Holy Spirit in the Pauline Letters." *Interpretation,* Vol. 33 (Jan. 1979), pp. 3–18.

Nelson, J. Robert. "The Holy Spirit: Personal, Ecclesial, Mundane." *Religion in Life,* Vol. 48 (Summer 1979), pp. 203–216.

Ramsey, Michael. *Jesus and the Living Past.* Oxford University Press, 1980.

2. THE DIVINITY OF THE SPIRIT

Bracken, Joseph A. "Process Philosophy and Trinitarian Theology." *Process Studies,* Vol. 8 (Winter 1978), pp. 217–230.

――――. *What Are They Saying About the Trinity?* Paulist Press, 1979.

Engelsman, Joan Chamberlain. *The Feminine Dimension of the Divine.* Westminster Press, 1979.

Hendry, George S. *The Holy Spirit in Christian Theology.* Revised and enlarged edition. Westminster Press, 1965.

Moltmann, Jürgen. *The Crucified God.* Harper & Row, 1974.

———. *The Trinity and the Kingdom*. Harper & Row, 1981.

Nielsen, Charles M. "How to Teach the Trinity in an Age of Academic and Social Disorder." *Religion in Life*, Vol. 43 (Autumn 1974), pp. 306–310.

Opsahl, Paul D., ed. *The Holy Spirit in the Life of the Church*. Augsburg Publishing House, 1978.

Pagels, Elaine H. *The Gnostic Gospels*. Random House, 1979.

Panikkar, Raimundo. *The Trinity and the Religious Experience of Man*. Orbis Books, 1973.

Pelikan, Jaroslav. *The Emergence of the Catholic Tradition (100-600)*. University of Chicago Press, 1971. Vol. 1 of The Christian Tradition.

Pittenger, Norman. "God 'The One in Three, the Three in One.' " *Religion in Life*, Vol. 48 (Spring 1979), pp. 93–100.

Russell, Letty M. *The Future of Partnership*. Westminster Press, 1979.

Tennis, Diane. "The Loss of the Father God: Why Women Rage and Grieve." *Christianity and Crisis*, Vol. 41 (June 8, 1981), pp. 164–170.

Welch, Claude. *In This Name: The Doctrine of the Trinity in Contemporary Theology*. Charles Scribner's Sons, 1952.

3. THE HOME OF THE SPIRIT

Brown, Robert McAfee. "No Faith Is an Island." *The Christian Century*, Vol. 90 (Feb. 27, 1974), pp. 229–231.

Kraus, C. Norman. *The Community of the Spirit*. Wm. B. Eerdmans Publishing Co., 1974.

Nutall, Geoffrey F. *The Holy Spirit in Puritan Faith and Experience*. Macmillan Co., 1947.

Rahner, Karl. *The Spirit in the Church*. Seabury Press, 1979.

Roy, Rustum. *Experimenting with Truth*. Oxford: Pergamon Press, 1981.

Winn, Albert Curry. "The Holy Spirit and the Christian Life." *Interpretation*, Vol. 33 (Jan. 1979), pp. 47–57.

4. THE LANGUAGE OF THE SPIRIT

Buechner, Frederick. *Wishful Thinking: A Theological ABC*. Harper & Row, 1973.

Neusner, Jacob. *The Glory of God Is Intelligence.* Salt Lake City: Publishers Press, 1978.

Nouwen, Henri J. M. "Compassion: The Core of Spiritual Leadership." *Occasional Papers: Institute for Ecumenical and Cultural Research,* March 1977, pp. 1–6.

5. THE GIFTS OF THE SPIRIT

Berkhof, Hendrikus. *The Doctrine of the Holy Spirit.* John Knox Press, 1964.

Brown, Schuyler. " 'Water-Baptism' and 'Spirit-Baptism' in Luke-Acts." *Anglican Theological Review,* Vol. 59 (April 1977), pp. 135–150.

Bruner, Frederick Dale. *A Theology of the Holy Spirit: The Pentecostal Experience and the New Testament Witness.* Wm. B. Eerdmans Publishing Co., 1970.

Cobb, John B., Jr. *Theology and Pastoral Care.* Fortress Press, 1977.

Edwards, Jonathan. *The Great Awakening.* Ed. by C. C. Goen. Yale University Press, 1972. Vol. 4 of The Works of Jonathan Edwards.

Haughey, John C. *The Conspiracy of God.* Doubleday & Co., 1973.

Wilson-Kastner, Patricia. *Coherence in a Fragmented World: Jonathan Edwards' Theology of the Holy Spirit.* University Press of America, 1978.

6. THE ECSTASY OF THE SPIRIT

Bittlinger, Arnold. "Charismatic Renewal: An Opportunity for the Church." *Ecumenical Review,* Vol. 31 (July 1979), pp. 247-251.

Green, Michael. *I Believe in the Holy Spirit.* Wm. B. Eerdmans Publishing Co., 1976.

Kinghorn, Kenneth Cain. *Fresh Wind of the Spirit.* Abingdon Press, 1975.

Suenens, Leon Joseph. *A New Pentecost?* Seabury Press, 1975.

The Work of the Holy Spirit: Report of the Special Committee on the Work of the Holy Spirit to the 182nd General Assembly, The United Presbyterian Church in the U.S.A. New York: Office of the General Assembly, 1970.

Yankelovich, Daniel. *New Rules.* Random House, 1981.

7. THE SCOPE OF THE SPIRIT

Berger, Peter. *The Heretical Imperative: Contemporary Possibilities of Religious Affirmation*. Doubleday & Co., Anchor Press Book, 1979.

Burkle, Howard R. "Jesus Christ and Religious Pluralism." *Journal of Ecumenical Studies*, Vol. 16 (Spring 1979), pp. 457–471.

Davis, Stephen T. "Evangelicals and the Religions of the World." *Reformed Journal*, Vol. 31 (June 1981), pp. 9–13.

Elmen, Paul. "Scandalizing the Little Ones." *The Christian Century*, Vol. 98 (March 25, 1981), pp. 324–327.

Faricy, Robert. "Nature, Social Sin, and the Spirit." In Edward Malatesta, ed. *The Spirit of God in Christian Life*. Paulist Press, 1977.

Fries, Paul R. "God's Human Face: Reflections on Spirit, Kingdom, and Culture." *Reformed Journal*, Vol. 30 (Oct. 1980), pp. 10–14.

Henry, Patrick. "Religion and Art: The Uneasy Alliance." *Religion in Life*, Vol. 49 (Winter 1980), pp. 448–460.

Hick, John. "Pluralism and the Reality of the Transcendent." *The Christian Century*, Vol. 97 (Jan. 21, 1981), pp. 45–48.

⸺, ed. *Truth and Dialogue in World Religions*. Westminster Press, 1974.

MacKinnon, Donald. *Borderlands of Theology, and Other Essays*. Edited and introduced by George W. Roberts and Donovan E. Smucker. London: Lutterworth Press, 1968.

Moule, C. F. D. *The Holy Spirit*. Oxford: A. R. Mowbray & Co., 1978; Grand Rapids, Mich.: Wm. B. Eerdmans Publishing Co., 1979.

Pittenger, Norman. *The Holy Spirit*. United Church Press, Pilgrim Press Book, 1974.

Rahner, Karl. *Meditations on Freedom and the Spirit*. Seabury Press, 1978.

Ramsey, Michael. *Holy Spirit: A Biblical Study*. Wm. B. Eerdmans Publishing Co., 1978.

Taylor, John V. *The Go-Between God: The Holy Spirit and the Christian Mission*. Oxford University Press, 1979.

Warren, Max. *I Believe in the Great Commission*. Wm. B. Eerdmans Publishing Co., 1976.

Wingren, Gustaf. *Credo: The Christian View of Faith and Life*. Augsburg Publishing House, 1981.